GROW

How to Take Your DIY Project & Passion to the Next Level and Quit Your Job!

GROW

*How to Take Your DIY Project & Passion
to the Next Level and Quit Your Job!*

Eleanor C. Whitney

Released June 1, 2013
Second Printing, July 2013
ISBN 978-1-62106-007-9

Cover by Meggyn Pomerleau
Designed by Meggyn Pomerleau with Joe Biel
Edited by Joe Biel and Lauren Hage

Distributed by IPG, Chicago and Turnaround, UK

Microcosm Publishing
636 SE 11th Ave.
Portland, OR 97214

www.microcosmpublishing.com

GROW

How to Take Your DIY Project & Passion to the Next Level and Quit Your Job!

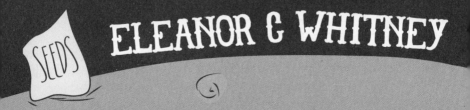

SEEDS

ELEANOR C WHITNEY

T

INTRODUCTION 7

CHAPTER 1: GET CLEAR AND GET GROWING 10

On a Mission **12**
Be Goal Oriented **15**
Time is of the Essence **17**
Ground Rules for Do-It-Yourself Entrepreneurs from
      Amy Cuevas Schroeder **18**
Profile: Building a healthy, Successful DIY Project with
      Filmmaker William E. Badgley **20**
Chapter One Checklist **21**

**CHAPTER 2: BE A CREATIVE MONEY MAKER: FIND
AND CREATE THE RESOURCES YOU NEED 22**

Assess your Feelings about Money **24**
Tell the Story of Your Project in Numbers:
      Make a Budget **25**
Expenses: What Will You Spend? **26**
Income: What Will You Bring In? **28**
In-Kind Support **28**
Bartering **29**
Earned Income: Pricing Your Work **30**
Earned Income: Paying Yourself **32**
Nothing is Certain Except... Taxes **36**
Raising Money **37**
Fundraising Campaign Planning **38**
Organizing Fundraising Events **40**
Growing Support from Individuals **42**
Crowd-Funding **43**
Fundraising 101: Raising Money From
      Grants **45**
Nonprofit Status and Fiscal Sponsorship **48**
Applying For Grants **49**
Build a Healthy Relationship with Money **52**
Chapter 2 Checklist **54**

A

B

L

E

O

F

CHAPTER 3: BUILDING COMMUNITY AND SPREADING THE WORD: DO IT YOURSELF MARKETING, IDENTITY AND MEDIA 55

Market Research: Who Needs Your Project? **57**
Identify Yourself **58**
Develop Your Pitch **60**
Cultivating Personal Connections Through Outreach **61**
Your Presence on the Web **63**
Social Media Guidelines **66**
Selling Handmade Items and Building Community Online **68**
Press Outreach: Engaging Traditional Media **69**
Planning a Press Campaign **70**
Press Outreach Guidelines **72**
Tools for Effective Press Outreach **73**
Marketing is Community Building **74**
Chapter 3 Checklist **75**

CHAPTER 4: DIY BUSINESS SENSE: WHAT YOU NEED TO KNOW TO GROW 76

Profile: Starting a Handmade Business: Brooklyn Soda Works **78**
Questions to Ask when Starting a Handmade Business **78**
Setting up Your Business **79**
Small Business Lessons from Punk Rope **80**
Tips for Deciding on a Business Entity **81**
Types of Business **82**
Profile: threewalls gallery: Building a Small, Sustainable Creative Nonprofit **84**
Licenses, Taxes, Permits, Zoning, and Insurance **86**
Protect Your Relationships and Creations: Memorandum of Understanding, Contracts, and Intellectual Property **87**
Contract Basics **88**
Protect Your Intellectual Property **89**
Copyright and Trademark 101 **90**
Fair Use **91**
Conclusion: Know What You Need to Grow **92**
Chapter 4 Checklist **92**

CONTENTS

CHAPTER 5: BUILDING A DIY LIFE 93

Nurture Healthy Work Habits **95**
Make Your Project a Priority in Your Life **96**
Keep Your Project in Perspective **98**
Build Healthy Collaborations **99**
Nurture DIY Community **102**
Four Elements of a Successful, DIY
                    Community Project **104**
Organizing and Running a Collective:
Sarah Evans and the Roberts Street
                    Social Centre **105**
The Business of DIY: Are you Ready to
        Do- It-Yourself Full-time? **107**
Letting Your Business Grow **110**
Guidelines for Sustainable DIY Business
                    Growth **110**
Reflect, Reassess, and Stay Motivated **112**
The Life Cycle of a Project **113**
Considerations for Ending or Shifting a
                    Project **115**
Tips for Building Your DIY Project,
                Business and Life **116**
Embrace Your DIY Present and Future.
                Dare to Grow **117**

RESOURCES 119

ACKNOWLEDGEMENTS 126

ABOUT THE AUTHOR 127

INTRODUCTION

 "Go DIY!" is stenciled on the floor of my parents' basement. It is left behind from a silkscreen project I did in the late nineties when I made patches to stitch on my messenger bag to share my love of do it yourself culture with the world. To me DIY represented empowerment, creative potential, and the ability to make my life how I wanted it to be. I still have the silkscreen and, fifteen years later, I'm still enamored with DIY culture and the impact it has on peoples' lives and society as a whole.

Do It Yourself culture is reshaping the way we work, think, and create. The DIY community is made up of enterprising people from all backgrounds and at all points in their lives who have decided to engage their ingenuity and passion to pursue the project or business of their dreams.

When you join the DIY community and invest time, energy, and money into a personal, creative project that reflects your vision and values, you take a leap into the unknown. Doing-it-yourself means you rely on your own ambition, motivation, and skills to make your vision a reality. But just because you are determined to do it yourself doesn't mean you have to do it alone.

Grow is a starting point. Its mission is to serve as a resource for creative people, such as yourself, who have great ideas for independent projects in all mediums, including publishing, music, food, art, craft, activism, or community work. It will enable you to clarify your vision, get organized, create a plan, raise funds for, market, and manage your do it yourself project. *Grow* will enable you to harness your enthusiasm and innovative ideas to create a successful, sustainable project in a supportive community.

Grow will connect you with the information and resources that you need to take your project to the next level, whether that's completing your first zine or launching the business of your dreams that will enable you to quit your job. The people and businesses profiled in this book have succeeded in doing just that and have shared what they have learned with you. Throughout the book I've also shared my own stories and lessons I learned from involvement with the do it yourself community.

When I got the idea for *Grow* I envisioned a resource that would help creative, inspiring people make their do it yourself projects a reality. I imagined a future where creative people who are invested in the ethics and energy of the do it yourself community could access needed skills and resources to find success. I imagined a supportive community of creative people who were able to actualize and sustain their vision in the long term.

This book will support you through the life of your project from the first brainstorm to its successful conclusion.

- **Chapter One** walks you through the basics of defining you project, articulating a mission and project goals and setting up a timeline.

- **Chapter Two** focuses on finding the monetary and non-monetary resources you need and introduces you to the financial basics of budgeting, earning money, and fundraising.

- **Chapter Three** explains how to create an identity for your project, get the word out about it, and navigate the world of outreach, marketing, and social media.

- **Chapter Four** shows you how to build your business DIY style and introduces you to basic business structures and how to protect your project through contracts and copyright.

- **Chapter Five** brings all of these ideas together and explains how to build a holistic, successful, sustainable DIY life. It features guidelines for how to take care of yourself, nurture DIY community and build healthy partnerships and collaborations so your project can grow with your dreams.

The back of the book contains a resource section that includes my favorite books, organizations, and websites that you can access to help channel your passion and creativity into successful, sustainable projects and be a powerful tool for cultural and social change.

This book is deeply personal to me. DIY has been a part of my life since I was a child and my parents taught me to make my own clothes and grow my own vegetables, and I launched an organic gardening business. The ideas to write *Grow* grew out of my fifteen-year involvement with punk, feminist, and independent art communities. As a teenager the idea of do it yourself seemed infinitely logical because I loved to write and play music and was passionate about social justice and feminism. At the time I understood that as a teenager no "real" publisher or record label would take me seriously. "Why should I wait for someone else?" I asked myself. I started a personal zine, launched a record and cassette label, and co-founded a Riot Grrrl inspired group for young feminists in my hometown of Portland, Maine.

Since then I have published zines, helped found and run the annual Portland Zine Symposium, played and toured with indie rock bands, edited a queer, feminist art journal, wrote a food blog and hosted artisanal food events, and worked as a media and art educator, programmer, and administrator. With *Grow* I want to share what I have learned with others who take their ideas seriously and are building a creative, independent life.

This book reflects my vision for supportive communities where people are creatively fulfilled, economically stable, and able to build healthy, balanced lives on their own terms. It's a big vision, but I know that together we can make it happen.

The advice in *Grow* comes from my experiences, education and research, as well as interviews with creative people who have built inspiring projects, businesses and lives in the DIY spirit. Think of this book as your guide and companion to creating the project, life and business that you dream of. Your life and ideas belong to you and I can't wait to hear about what you make of them.

I've learned to recognize the feeling when an idea strikes, whether it's while I'm riding my bike to work, in the shower, at an event, or in the midst of a conversation. My stomach drops, my hands tingle, and my mind starts to race. I know that this idea is one worth perusing. This is an idea for a project, an event or group that will respond to a need and fulfill a personal passion. When I recognize an idea like this I feel a sense of urgency and a sense of responsibility to actualize it.

You know the feeling well: You have a project that you are so excited to work on and it keeps you up at night. You know that society needs to be changed and you have a way to change it. You've just been struck by inspiration or you have been nurturing a plan for a long time. Either way, you are ready to take action and make your vision a reality. You are ready to change the world with your project.

When you start a do it yourself project you empower yourself and take charge of your life while you work to make something concrete from your creative vision. When you take on a do it yourself project you bring an entrepreneurial spirit into your life. Amy Cuevas Schroeder, the founder of the DIY Business Association, explains, "Entrepreneurship at its heart is starting from nothing and creating a business. You have to engage your creativity when you start a DIY business or project because there's not one set formula for creating a business from scratch."

This chapter will help you take the big leap to begin to build your project and focus your creative energy. It will guide you through the process of making a mission statement, defining goals and action steps, and setting project deadlines. When you have a mission, goals, and a timeline for your project you lay the groundwork for success and create a firm foundation on which to grow.

Start now, where you are

Moving a project from idea to reality is exciting and daunting. Take advantage of the inspiration and energy you feel when you have a new idea to move forward.

To start, ask yourself a few simple questions.

- Can you describe your project in one sentence?

- What details do you know already about your project?

- What do you want to achieve? Is it a brand new project or have you been working on it for a long time and are ready to expand or take it in a new direction?

- How much do you know about what your project entails? Are you a complete beginner? An expert? Somewhere in the middle?

- Do you have a community of friends and family that know about— and support—your project?

While the idea of describing your project clearly and concisely may sound like a simple place to start, it is one of the most challenging parts of the process. When you understand deeply and clearly what you will create you can begin your project with focus and determination.

ON A MISSION

Step 1: envision success

Ask yourself: what do you want to achieve with your project? What is your ultimate vision of success? Engage your imagination and think big. For a moment, forget the practical and allow yourself to daydream. Imagine what success looks and feels like and record this vision in a way you can easily revisit. For example, write it down in a journal, sketch it on a piece of paper, or scribble it on post-it notes and stick them to your wall. Pretend that your project is finished and it has been successful. What have you created?

For example, if you have a desire to play in a band, imagine what success for your band means. Imagine that you have recorded an album that is well received and have gone on tour. How does that make you feel? From a broad vision like this you can focus into a specific mission statement to guide you through the creative process.

When I was working with a group of people to launch the Portland Zine Symposium over a decade ago we imagined a weekend full of workshops, social events, time and space to trade zines, and meeting other independent publishers that highlighted Portland, Oregon's dynamic, creative, DIY culture. We compared notes about other zine-focused events we had been to, what we liked and didn't, and imagined creating an event that was as strong, well-regarded, and as unique as Portland itself. From there we were able to focus on exactly what we wanted to do to achieve our vision.

Step 2: Craft a mission statement

A mission statement is a clear, to-the-point statement that helps define and guide a company, organization or project. It sums up in a few sentences the vision of the project's creator, what they hope to achieve, and outlines in the broadest terms how they will achieve it.

Mission statements for organizations and people profiled in this book communicate succinctly and powerfully what they have set out to achieve:

threewalls is an organization dedicated to increasing Chicago's cultural capital by cultivating contemporary art practice and discourse. Through a range of exhibition and public programs, including symposiums, lectures, performances and publications, threewalls creates a locus of exchange between local, national and international contemporary art communities.

The **INDEPENDENT PUBLISHING RESOURCE CENTER'S** mission is to facilitate creative expression, identity and community by providing individual access to tools and resources for creating independently published media and artwork.

BROOKLYN SODA WORKS sums up their business philosophy by describing what they make: We carbonate fresh fruit juice. We never use syrups or fruit concentrates - we juice everything by hand, and use local, seasonal fruit whenever possible... Our focus is on creating inventive new flavors and utilizing seasonal fruits and herbs. Sustainable produce is sourced from local farms whenever possible.

Kelly Carambula articulated a mission for her magazine **REMEDY QUARTERLY**: We believe that food is something that brings people together. Everyone has a story to tell, and more often than not, food is involved.

Remedy Quarterly gives people, whether professional food writers or top-notch grandmas, a place to share their stories and recipes, much like the community cookbooks that inspired us. Each issue has a theme and comes packed with stories and each of those comes with a recipe; most are delicious, some are hilarious.

Each of these mission statements make the purpose of the organization or project clear and summarizes what they do and why.

Your mission statement should be concise, memorable, far-reaching, and practical. It articulates the purpose of your project: what you want achieved, why you are doing it, and how. Your mission statement should give you a rush of inspiration and focus each time you read it.

Drafting and crafting a mission statement is a process. When I was in the Radical Art Girls collective in Portland, Oregon we spent a month trying to define our mission. We knew our mission needed to be snappy and bold, and that we all cared about feminism, art, and social change, but it was difficult to bring everyone's ideas together into a concise statement. We spent a long time discussing our goals and core values and how those were distinct from our overall mission. For example, was it necessary to include the importance of environmentally sustainable art in our mission? Or was that a value? After weeks of brainstorming and heated discussion we arrived at a simple mission and definition statement, "The Radical Art Girls are a mixed gender collective of young, feminist artists making art with political, personal, and social relevance." Our statement was supported by a longer list of core values such as, "Collective action, education, art, and decision making can and will transform society." While they were sometimes tedious, these discussions had the added benefit of bringing us closer as a collective.

Before you write your mission statement look at the mission statements for organizations you admire. Do they seem understandable or off the mark given what you know about that organization?

To draft your mission statement, try the following exercises:

- Describe your project or organization in 5 seconds. Write it down
- Describe your organization or project in 30 seconds. Write it down
- In one sentence what does your organization or project do?
- List three core values that drive your project or organization
- Articulate the impact you will have in the world: Write down your vision of success

Use these brainstorming exercises to create a paragraph-long draft of your mission statement. Read draft statement out loud. Make sure the language flows and that you have accurately captured your vision. Show a draft of your mission statement to friends and ask for their feedback. Keep revising your mission statement until it fully encompasses your vision.

You can publicize your mission statement to tell people about your project or keep it to yourself. It is a tool you can refer back to often in order to keep yourself on track and remind yourself what you are working to achieve. Revisit your mission statement regularly and don't be afraid to revise it if you find there's an element that no longer fits.

BE GOAL ORIENTED

Step 1: Define your big goals

Setting goals makes your mission statement concrete. Goals are precise statements about what you will achieve and are focused on results. Goals can be practical and audacious. The goals you set should inspire you to action. When you set bold goals they can push you beyond your comfort zone and help you achieve a new level of success with your project.

To start out set three to four big goals. Your project is manageable when you have a limited number of goals. Make each goal distinct and ensure that each one relates back to your mission statement. Goals start with action verbs, which make the reader feel motivated, focused, and excited to achieve them.

For example, if you are starting a band whose mission is to be a powerful, feminist rock group that combines politics and music, your goals could be:

- Write twelve songs and record an album

- Book and play six shows by the end of the year

- Support and volunteer for a local cause dedicated to women's rights

If your mission is to be the premiere e-shop for handmade, plus size, vintage inspired dresses you goals could be:

- Develop a line of three to five dresses that range from casual to dressy

- Become a trusted "go to" place to shop for your customers by making them look and feel good

- Advocate for a vision of fashion and style that is inclusive of women of all sizes

As you set goals revisit your big vision of success. You can set goals that are very simple, but dare to push yourself. As you achieve your goals, you'll set new ones. Once you have your big goals defined you need to break them into smaller, achievable steps to help you along your way.

Step 2: Break your goals into action steps

Once you have your big goals defined it is time to get practical. Break each of your goals into specific action steps that will help you achieve them. For example, if one of your goals is to record an album, first you have to write songs. An action step could be to write a certain number of songs by a certain date. These smaller, action oriented steps act like mile markers along the way to reaching your big goal. They keep your project on track and give you a feeling of accomplishment and motivation when you achieve them.

Concrete action steps create a road map to success. Depending on the size and complexity of your big goals you might need to break your action steps into still smaller subtasks. To do this ask yourself, "What needs to be done to accomplish my goal?" Write all of these tasks down. Then organize these tasks into a list in the order they need to be accomplished. As you work on your project this order may change and you may add and subtract tasks, but having a list of bite-sized tasks will enable you to work methodically towards your goal.

Since I graduated from college I have been pursuing a goal of becoming a professional, nonfiction writer who focuses on art, culture, politics, food, creativity, and personal story telling. To achieve this overall goal I broke it down into small, attainable steps, such as: identify websites and publications that reflected my interests and who would accept submissions, and publish one piece per month in each of my areas of interests. When I achieve an action step, such as making a connection with a new editor and completing another piece, I feel concrete progress towards my ambitious goal.

TIME IS OF THE ESSENCE

Step 1: Set up your timeline

When do you want to achieve your ultimate goal? How long will your action steps and supporting tasks take to complete? A timeline will guide you and deadlines will enable you to keep your project on track. It is an essential tool when you are balancing your project with the rest of your life.

Without a concrete timeline and deadlines it can be difficult to achieve your goals, even if you have already put in the effort to create your project. For example, my band Corita had recorded our first EP and made it available online. Our friends and fans kept asking us when we would have a CD or record they could get from us at shows. We told them, "When we have time to make one," which we never did. It wasn't until we were booked to play shows during the South by Southwest (SXSW) festival in Austin, Texas that we realized we needed to have copies of our EP to give out because people were not going to go online to hear our music. When we had the looming deadline of a trip all the way to Texas we finally made the time to get together to make CDs and therefore achieved one of our goals: to make our music available for people to hear outside of coming to a show.

When you are working out your timeline give yourself the time you need to achieve your goals. Account for other activities and events in your life. Are you graduating from school or taking a major trip? Do you have a job that gets busy during a certain time of year? Be honest about your other time commitments to keep your project on track. Talk with your friends and family about your schedule and get their feedback. When you are realistic about your timeframe you also avoid getting discouraged. Many of us are overly ambitious and want to say we can achieve more than is possible in the time that we have. Give yourself enough time to complete your project to ensure a quality result, but be sure that your deadlines are tight enough that they keep you motivated.

Step 2: Find the tools that help you stay on track

Use the tools that work for you to plan your timeline whether it's an electronic calendar or good old paper calendar. You can make a storyboard or a series of drawings to illustrate your timeline. Whatever tools you use make sure that they are easy and accessible so that you can track your progress and keep yourself accountable to the deadlines that you set up. Revise your timeline as you achieve your intermediate goals and get a better sense of how long the different elements of your project take.

GROUND RULES FOR DO-IT-YOURSELF ENTREPRENEURS FROM AMY CUEVAS SCHROEDER

Amy Cuevas Schroeder founded the DIY Business Association, which provides events and content to empower and connect creative entrepreneurs and believes it takes a community to do it yourself. She got her entrepreneurial start in the mid-'90s when she founded Venus Zine, the magazine for women in music and DIY culture, at age 19. She grew the publication into an internationally circulated magazine. She works for Etsy as a content specialist for their Seller Handbook and blogs about DIY entrepreneurship, life in Brooklyn, and her projects at thevenuslady.com

Set guidelines for yourself to help ensure the success of your project:

- Be a motivated self-starter

- Know your strengths and weakness. What are you really good at?

- Define your level of commitment upfront. Be honest about how much time you have to give and what you need from others

- Be a collaboration artist and find creative ways to work together with people

- Subscribe to the theory of what goes around comes around. You are going to have to help others because you will rely on them to help you

- Respect that leadership comes in all shapes, ages and sizes

- Pivot and try new ideas if something is not working

- Ask good questions and do the background research

- Most important, start where you are

PROFILE: BUILDING A HEALTHY, SUCCESSFUL DIY PROJECT WITH FILMMAKER WILLIAM E. BADGLEY

Filmmaker William E. Badgley is the director of the film *Kill All Redneck Pricks: A Documentary Film about a Band Called KARP*, which follows the story of a do it yourself rock band from Tumwater, Washington in the 1990s.

William is also a musician, and has been playing guitar in the band Federation X for over fourteen years. He found that playing in a punk band was excellent preparation for becoming a filmmaker and pursuing a creative career path because creativity, according to Badgley, "When you are working on a creative project, like a band or a film, you can't just clock out at the end of the day like a job. It is a responsibility that never leaves you."

To build a sustainable project:

- Be in love with your project

- Your project is an entity that is both creative and financial. Make both as healthy and beautiful as you can

- Tailor your life towards your project. Know what creature comforts you need to compromise in order to find focus and resources for your project

- Identify the ideas that scare you and take concrete steps to actualize them. Those ideas will lead you down your true path

- Make a plan for creating the project that includes taking care of yourself

- Find the match between your personal passion and what the public desires. That's smart business

- When collaborating with others be clear the role each person will play

CHAPTER 1 CHECKLIST

- Write a mission to clarify the sense of purpose for your project. What will your project achieve?

- Define big project goals that are directly related to your mission. Be clear about what will you create and define action steps to support each goal.Ensure that those action steps are realistic, concrete, and achievable.

- Create a timeline for your project. Determine how long it will take you to accomplish the goals and action steps you have mapped out. Use the date tracking tools that work best for you to keep yourself on top of project deadlines.

- Be confident and committed to your project in order to work through doubts

- Success means surviving the mistakes that you make

- Bring common sense to your project—it is your skills and organization that will carry a project through

When the big ideas for a project are clear, engaging your creativity and jumping into the unknown is less scary. When you spend the time to define a mission, set goals and make a timeline you will be prepared to tackle the practical and logistical aspects of your project with focus and grace. Set ground rules to put yourself in the right mind frame to create and reach out to your friends and family to build a community around you that supports your creativity. When you have these elements in place the easiest next step is to get growing.

CHAPTER 2

BE A CREATIVE MONEY MAKER:
FIND AND CREATE THE RESOURCES YOU NEED

"**M**oney is nothing more than the ability to do what you want to do. If you are a good person you will do good with it," said filmmaker and musician William E. Badgley.

Taking control of your finances will enable you to take control of your creative process. Knowing how much money you need to create your project means that you will be able to assess what resources you need, and make a plan to secure them.

You are likely embarking on your do it yourself project out of a sense of passion and dedication, along with an excitement to accomplish something new and different. Despite the fact that many go the do it yourself route to save money, finances are still a consideration—even for projects that are nonprofit, community oriented, or anti-capitalist.

Despite being the symbol of status in western culture, few people talk about money honestly. Avoiding the subject of money will not help your project develop. Being realistic about project costs from the beginning will enable you have a practical approach to project finances.

Creating a financial plan will empower you to feel confident about finding resources for your project. It will also help you avoid unexpected costs that can stall your project or put you in debt. Jessica Hopper breaks down the importance of connecting your goals, mission, and timeline to your finances in her article *Be Your Own Boss* for *Rookie Magazine*. "You need a business plan: a clear idea of what you're doing and how you'll make money (or at least how you'll avoid losing money)."

Christen Carter, Founder and CEO of Busy Beaver Buttons, found that focusing on finance made her feel free to innovate and grow her business. "I thought that focusing on the numbers would take away from the creativity, but it actually added to the creative process in ways I never expected," she said. "Numbers are exciting. They are proof of what you are doing right, what you should continue to do, and what you should change."

When I went to graduate school to get my Master's in Public Administration I was required to take budgeting, finance, and economics classes. At first I dreaded them, but to my surprise I found that they were my favorite part of school. I realized that thinking about numbers in the context of a project I wanted to accomplish was exciting and empowering.

Let's talk about how to put yourself in the right financial frame of mind; how to build a meaningful budget for your project; cover the basics of selling your work and pricing your time; and introduce fundraising strategies such as crowd-funding, benefit events, and grants.

Once your finances are in order you will be freed up to work towards your greatest goals, like quitting your day job and building the life you want with confidence.

ASSESS YOUR FEELINGS ABOUT MONEY

The first step in creating a financial plan for your project is to understand your own relationship to money. Is there a part of you that wants to run away screaming as soon as you hear the words "money," or "finance?" Or, are you a careful budgeter who already tracks your personal expenses?

I used to groan internally and stop listening whenever the word "money" or "budget" was brought up in relation to a creative or activist project. I thought that if I had a compelling vision, strong passion, and put a lot of work into my project, the money and resources I needed would naturally follow. When I helped found the Portland Zine Symposium in 2001 I did not think about money or a budget for the event. I assumed we could find what we needed for free. We were lucky to be surrounded by a very generous and enthusiastic community who recognized we were taking on a big project for the first time and rallied to support us. We managed to scramble up a few last minute dollars through bake sales and benefit shows, but also found out the hard way that many businesses that wanted to donate to us could only do so if we were registered as or sponsored by a nonprofit. After the first Symposium was over we realized that if we were going to make it a sustainable, annual event we would need to know how much it would cost to put on. If we knew the cost we could be realistic in what we could and could not offer to participants and we would no longer run the risk of wearing out our welcome with community members that offered us their time, energy, and resources.

Before you dive in to create a budget for your project, set prices for the products you produce, hire people to work with you, pay yourself, and start raising money, take a few minutes, or hours, to reflect on these questions:

- Do you have a personal or project budget?

    o   Do you follow it? Why or why not?

    o   How diligent are you in tracking your day-to-day expenses?

- Think about your financial history:

    o   What are your proudest achievements?

    o   What are big financial lessons you learned the hard way?

    o   Do you see a pattern or repeated mistakes?

- In your opinion, what is good about money?

- What specifically about money makes you anxious?

It can be scary to look yourself (and your bank account) straight in the eye and acknowledge your weaknesses, but you might also find that you have stronger financial skills than you thought. Often the most important skill is having confidence. When you know where you need to grow, and where you are strong financially, you can take a proactive stance to tackle your project's budget and finances.

TELL THE STORY OF YOUR PROJECT IN NUMBERS: MAKE A BUDGET

When you make a budget you take the first step towards understanding and taking control of your project's finances. You don't need to force yourself to be familiar with accounting jargon to take this part of the project. Creating a project budget can be straightforward: it simply requires thinking about your project in terms of expenses and income to understand what resources are coming in and going out.

Your budget supports your project's mission, goals, and timeline by breaking down what the resources you will need and attaching costs to them. At graduate school my budgeting and finance professor, Martha Stark, cut through the fog of mystery around budgets and told us simply, "A budget tells the story of your project, your business, or your life in numbers."

EXPENSES: WHAT WILL YOU SPEND?

When you have a clear vision for your project, making your budget will be a simple next step.

Start your expense budget with a brainstorm. Make a list of everything you need to accomplish with your project. Do you need a particular type of material or equipment? Do you need to rent a space? Hire someone with a specialized skill? Pay for postage or travel? Most importantly, you may need to pay yourself.

Once your list is complete, organize it into broad categories. Group similar expenses together, for example: paint, brushes, ladders, and drop cloths for your mural painting project could go under "Supplies," whereas the website, posters, and invitations that you will send to promote the mural's opening could be grouped together under "Publicity."

Once your expenses are organized into **categories**, format your budget in a spreadsheet. Spreadsheets are important, even for simple

EXPENSES	Expense Breakdown	Totals
SUPPLIES		
Paint	$300	
Hardware	$300	
Supplies Total		$600
PUBLICITY		
Website design and hosting	$400	
Poster printing	$200	
Invitation printing	$150	
Publicity Total		$750
STAFF		
Artist's Fee	$500	
Artist's Assistant	$250	
Staff Total		$750
TOTAL EXPENSES		$2100

Here is a basic example from the mural project.

project budgets. They can easily perform functions like adding columns of numbers and calculating percentages. Take a few hours to learn the basics of using spreadsheets—there are free online tutorials available to help you. Use formulas to save you from entering the same information over and over.

Once your expenses are organized into a **spreadsheet** it's time to attach specific costs to them. Put on your best bargain hunter and researcher hats and compare prices on the Internet and at local stores. Are you going to need a large amount of a particular material? Does it make sense to buy it in bulk or wholesale? Ask others who use similar supplies as you for their projects. Where do they get their materials?

Determine how much the services you need will cost. Ask different service providers, whether designers, web developers, lawyers, or accountants, whether they charge hourly or if they charge a flat fee for the service you need. Ask for references or recommendations before committing to hire someone.

Factor in how much to pay yourself and how much your time is worth. It is important to value your time as a creative person, even though you may not plan to make any money from your project at first. Your budget can be a plan for a time when your project has more money available to it. You should have an idea of how to compensate yourself for your time. There is more about this issue in the "Income" section later in this chapter.

As you **invest money in your project** be sure to save your receipts and keep a record of how much you are spending and on what. Filmmaker William E. Badgley admitted that he used to be afraid to pay attention to money because he feared it would crush the creativity of his projects, but he points out that, "If your bottom line is really small you should pay more attention to money, because you can't afford to make costly mistakes."

In doing your **pricing research** you may ask "But what if prices change? What if I need more or less of something than I thought?" Your initial budget is a prediction, not a determination, of what will happen in the future. Once your project begins you can compare actual expenses to your estimated expenses and adjust your budget accordingly. Knowing what you are spending makes it easier to plan for the future of the project.

INCOME: WHAT WILL YOU BRING IN?

Income is all resources that you find to support your project.

When you make an expense budget you only tell half the story of your project. To tell the rest you need to plan and budget for income. It's okay if your budget is a work of fiction until you start to bring in money and support for your project. But evaluating income at the beginning stage is important because it helps you focus on exactly how much money or support you need to make the project happen. To begin to think about income for your project, ask yourself the following questions:

- How do you expect your project to make money or support itself?
- Will you be doing all the work yourself? Trading goods or services with others? Asking for volunteers?
- Will you set aside part of your paycheck each month? Sell a product? Fundraise to cover your project's expenses?

At the beginning of the income planning process you may not know the answer to all of these questions, and your income can expand as the project develops. So let's think about the many ways you can find support for your project. Typical categories of income include: in-kind support, bartering, earning income through selling your work and charging for your time, and fundraising.

IN-KIND SUPPORT

Look at your budget and see what services or goods you could barter for or receive as "in-kind" support. In-kind support means that someone gives you a good or a service without charging you. If someone donates $100 worth of art supplies to your zine making class for school children that's $100 you don't have to spend out of your budget. If you are a nonprofit or have the ability to offer a tax-deduction in return for in-kind support be aware that the IRS only recognizes the donation of tangible goods, not services, as tax deductible.

BARTERING

Bartering is a powerful way to raise support for your project. Bartering builds good will and is mutually beneficial to both parties. Shana Brady of Punk Rope Fitness explains that, "If you take the time to support those in your community it will come back to you in some form. You can't put a price tag on those relationships."

Bartering goes beyond a simple trade among friends and is a specific, transactional relationship. Find members of your community that have a skill or resource that you need for your project and identify what you can offer them in return. For example, I have traded photos of my band for French lessons. The photographer and I worked out a specific number of lessons and the type of photos I would receive in advance. Like any transaction, it's important to put your barter agreement in writing to make sure everyone is clear about what to expect and what is expected in return. Bartering will also build knowledge and goodwill about your project beyond your immediate group of friends. To ensure a successful barter, follow these guidelines.

From Tim Haft and Shana Brady of Punk Rope Fitness

- Identify people who have the skills that you need. Go to the true experts

- Set realistic expectations of what you can offer and what its worth

- Be specific about the terms of the barter

- Be prepared for negotiation

- Examine the motivation of the person offering to barter

- Avoid one-sided arrangements that only benefit one party

- Be careful when bartering with friends and mixing business and social relationships

After you have made a plan for bartering and in-kind support you may find that you still need some cold, hard cash to make your project happen.

EARNED INCOME: PRICING YOUR WORK

Earned income is what we think of as "making money." It is money you receive from selling a product or a service. For example, a band generates earned income when they sell tickets, LPs, and t-shirts. Plan carefully about how much to charge for a product. Evaluate how much each one costs to make, the size of your audience, and how much they are willing to pay for what you are offering to them. When you have knowledge of price and audience you won't overestimate the amount of money you will make from sales or under price your work, which are two common mistakes I see creative people make often.

I used to charge $1 to $3 for my zine *Indulgence*, depending on how long it was and how much it cost me to mail and photocopy, because that's what everyone else changed for their zines. When I began to add fancy art papers, hand binding, and letterpress printing I was hesitant to charge more at first. I was afraid other zine makers in the community I was a part of would judge me for having a zine that was too expensive. However, when I finally raised my price to $5 the community was suddenly more interested in my fancier looking zines because they felt the price helped communicate the fact that that they were valuable and desirable.

So how do you determine your prices? For example, If your band usually draws 40 people and shows in your area usually cost $5 it would be reasonable to expect that you could bring in $200 from that show. Does $200 cover your expenses? Is your band popular enough that you could charge more? Or do you need to charge less to draw a larger audience? Look at the prices of projects like your own. How much are people willing to pay? How popular is a particular item?

Antonio Ramos from Brooklyn Soda Works lays out factors to consider when pricing your work, "What does it cost to make? How long does it take to make it? What profit can you make from your product at a price people will pay without compromising the essential nature of the project?"

Below are basic guidelines to follow when pricing your work:

- How much do the raw materials to make your item cost?

- How much time does it take to make your item? Your price should cover this time, including the time it took to create and refine the idea for your item. For example, a band would include the writing and rehearsal of a song.

- Know the standard price for your object, such as greeting cards or an album.

- How much are your customers willing to pay?

- How low of a price would make your customers decide your item is not worth their time?

- How valuable is your item? Choosing a price is about assigning a value, so you want to make sure you also don't over-value your creation or under-value yourself.

Refer to pricing guides if you work in a specific discipline, such as crafts, visual arts, or music. There is more information about where to find these in the Reference section. There's rarely a specific formula and the conventional wisdom about pricing varies depending on the discipline.

It is important to be confident when you talk about price. When asked how much a zine, record, cassette, or art book I made cost I used to shrug the question off as not important. I realized that when I approached my creation with that attitude I was treating my creative work as not important. I have readjusted my approach to represent my prices with confidence. When I trust that my work is worth the value I have assigned it I am also trusting that what I make is valuable.

Pricing terminology

In order be better able to discuss prices with buyers, suppliers, and retailers, and to build your confidence in the prices you set, it is helpful to be familiar with the following terms and ideas about pricing:

TOTAL COST TO PRODUCE YOUR ITEM is the cost of materials, labor, and time it takes for you to make one item. This should not be your price, but you should always be aware of and consider this number.

WHOLESALE PRICE is the price at which you offer your product to retailers. You will be offering your items to retailers at a "markup" price on your base cost. The markup should cover your overhead, such as your studio space and your tools. There's no hard and fast formula for determining the wholesale price, but it can range between 100 and 300 percent of the total cost, depending on the product you are offering.

RETAIL PRICE is the price you suggest to retailers to sell your item. This can be twice or even three times the wholesale price. Retailers take a percentage of the sale of your item to cover their costs. In addition, when you are selling your item yourself, such as through a website or at an event, you should offer it at the retail price.

There are no specific formulas for assigning a value to your work, but take time to research pricing strategies for your field and discuss with others who make similar work about how they set their prices. Most importantly, set out to cover your costs and feel good about your prices.

EARNED INCOME: PAYING YOURSELF

Paying yourself fairly for your work is an important step in building a sustainable, creative life. When you pay yourself you recognize the time and effort that goes into your work and acknowledge that your skills and expertise have value. Your craft's value is based on offering up your time, talents, or service—such as writing grant proposals, event planning, designing a website, or composing songs—rather than just producing a final product. Build confidence in yourself so that you can be compensated fairly.

Follow these guidelines as you work to set prices for the services you offer:

- Have the confidence to know that your time is worth money

- Set a clear goal of what you want to achieve with your project

- Clarify what you are selling. What is the exact service that you offer?

- Consider your experience and expertise. Do you have a perspective or level of experience that is not common for your field?

- What is the reward for the customer? How much value does what you're offering bring to your customers' lives?

Jessica Hopper, who ran a business as a music publicist, explains in an article in *Rookie* magazine that when she valued herself, others valued her as well. "I worked at cut-rate prices for years, despite being great at what I did, because I thought it was the punk thing to do and would instill loyalty. Neither of those things is true. At one point I found out what our competitors were charging and doubled my rates for all new business—and no one batted an eye."

Personally, learning to value my skills and myself enough to ask to be paid fairly has not been an easy process. I am lucky to do work I love such as teaching, writing, community organizing, and creative project management. Because I feel so passionate about these activities it was very easy for me to tell those interested in working with me, "Don't worry about the money. I just enjoy doing the work." When my to do list became too long and my calendar was full of other peoples' projects, I could not see a tangible benefit for me personally and realized that my commitments to other people took away from my time, energy, and enjoyment of my own projects. When I became confident enough to ask to be compensated for my time I was better able to judge what projects were worth it for me to take on. While it's great to contribute your time and energy to projects and initiatives you care deeply about, budget both of these carefully. When you take on new projects, whether paid or volunteer, be very clear about what benefit you are offering and what benefit you will receive.

Guidelines for pricing your time and services

There are no hard and fast formulas for determining how much to charge hourly or for project-based prices. However, there are strategies you can use to make an estimate and refine your prices from there. Musician Greta Gertler, who started Goldfish Prize PR to make an official business out of the networking, connecting, and outreach she was doing for musicians she loved, shared a simple strategy for pricing your time based on overhead costs and the amount of time you want to work.

Greta Gertler of Goldfish Prize PR's Pricing Strategy:

- Determine your overhead costs such as tools, software, studio rent, insurance, as well as living expenses for the year, month, and week

- Determine how many hours a week you want to work

- Divide these two numbers to determine your starting number for an hourly rate

For example:
$2,000 ÷ 4 = $500
$500 ÷ 30 = $17 basic hourly rate to cover expenses

Monthly Expenses	$2,000
Hours a week	30
Weeks in Month	4
Billable Hours in a week	15

However, you cannot bill your clients for every hour your spend working—they won't pay for you checking your email, networking, learning new skills, and everything else you do that is related to your project, but not the specific job they hired you to do. Thus your "billable" time should cover your expenses incurred during "non-billable" hours. Therefore, I may determine that I will work about 15 hours a week on my clients' specific projects, so I could raise my rate to $30 an hour to cover those expenses, so my calculations would look like this:

$2,000 ÷ 4 = $500
$500 ÷ 15 = $33 hourly rate to cover expenses for billable and non-billable time (I could raise or lower this rate to make a rounder number)

Once you have an idea of how much you need to charge to cover your expenses find out the going rate for your field. Talk to other professionals in your field about how they determine their prices. While it can feel awkward at first to talk about money, this is especially important when you are starting out. Build solidarity with those doing similar work to you. If you all are clear about what you charge there's a greater chance of being paid and treated fairly. Use general search terms on the Internet and check websites where freelancers advertise services or companies post ads looking for freelancers. Base your prices on these as a starting point.

Pricing Terms

These terms will enable you to discuss prices easily with those who are hiring you. Pricing your services can be done on a time basis, a project basis, or a package basis.

TIME-BASED is how much you charge per hour for your services. When you have an idea of your hourly rate you can determine the basis of what to charge for a specific project. Hourly rates are good for projects that take a fixed amount of time to accomplish, such as administrative support, installing an art piece, or outreach.

PROJECT-BASED is a price for an entire project that has a concrete end point, such as designing a brochure. When pricing based on a project, calculate how many hours it should take, as well as your overhead such as the tools and space you use to create it.

PACKAGE-BASED puts more conditions around a project, in the event that you manage additional consultations, revisions, or questions than you originally agreed upon. You offer a certain amount of time or number of consultations for a flat-fee and, if your client wants more changes or additional services, you can charge by the hour or an agreed-upon flat fee.

The key to pricing your services is to trust that your time is valuable and to communicate that value to others. You have skills, creativity, and expertise to offer to potential clients. If you are part of a community that is based on a barter economy be sure you explain clearly the time that it takes for you to make your product and make the expertise you bring to the service that you are offering clear. This will help ensure you get a fair trade. Be upfront about your needs. As a creative person educate yourself and your community members about your worth and do not work for less than you can afford to. You must value yourself before expecting anyone else to do so.

NOTHING IS CERTAIN EXCEPT... TAXES

As your project grows and you start making money from it the world of taxes quickly enters the picture. Taxes are an expense that you need to account for and are applicable once your project or business surpasses a hobby level. Accountants help ensure that the story you are telling about your project in numbers makes sense and can help you navigate the often-confounding world of taxes. Working with an accountant early on will guide you in determining what you owe in taxes, when you have to pay them, and how to deduct business related expenses from your tax bill. While they get a reputation as being boring number crunchers, accountants are an important member of your team. They are professionally trained to think about the rules and regulations that surround taxes and finances, which takes the guesswork out of dealing with taxes for you. When you have an accountant that you trust, you have peace of mind and are able to spend more time planning your project and less time worrying about money.

When do you have to pay taxes? Two basic scenarios can apply to do it yourself projects:

- When you sell goods online or in person, such as at a craft fair, you will need to collect sales tax. Sales tax rates vary by state, and state departments of finance have information on their website about how to register and collect sales tax.
- If you are working for yourself as a freelancer and are earning above a certain level, you may need to pay taxes quarterly. You can also deduct expenses related to your business activities.

To ensure you have everything you need to pay your taxes and deduct your expenses, save all receipts and invoices related to your project. Keep physical and digital copies and ensure that you know what a receipt is for and when that purchase was made. I'll admit it: it can be tedious to keep track of your expenses. Set aside a certain time every week that is dedicated to getting organized and putting your paperwork in order. Make a cup of coffee, put on a good record and organize your receipts. This will take some of the boredom and worry out of it.

When you are setting up a business or making the switch to working for yourself full time, it is a good idea to sit down with an accountant to discuss your tax situation. They can also offer you assistance to set up a book keeping and record system. This step will help you to have confidence that your project is on firm financial footing.

RAISING MONEY

Some projects need a greater amount of support than sales and bartering can cover. If your project is large scale, is based in benefiting a particular community, or you need to cover a large amount of start-up costs, raising funds and building community support for your project is another way to bring in income. Some ways you can do this are through fundraising events, individual giving campaigns, Internet-based crowd funding, and applying for grants.

"Just like do it yourself projects, raising money is about a personal touch and centers on building relationships with people," said Justin Hocking, the Executive Director of the Independent Publishing Resource Center. Fundraising is fundamentally not about money, but building a strong presence in a community. It is an area where you can use your creativity and careful planning to raise support to take your project to the next level.

When you fundraise you maintain control of your project. Caroline Mak, of Brooklyn Soda Works, explains, "You need access to cash to make a business run. For example, we need cash flow to be able to buy our ingredients every week. In seeking financial support we wanted to make sure we retained control of our company. Beware of loans with high interest rates and cast your net wide when looking for financing. The majority of small businesses are supported by family and friends."

FUNDRAISING CAMPAIGN PLANNING

Before you dive into planning a great fundraising campaign, know the basics of what you need, why you need it, who you will be asking for support, and how much time you have to fundraise. I've noticed that a lot of creative people, because they avoid talking about money, leave fundraising to the last minute. When you make a plan to raise money for your project you can have greater confidence that you can find the resources you need to make it happen. Take time to consider these questions so that you can build an exciting, beneficial fundraising campaign:

How Much?

How much money do you need to raise to cover your project expenses?
What will that money pay for?
Perhaps you have expensive materials to buy to begin making your project, or you are taking on a project that costs more than what you can save, barter, and earn income to support.

When?

What part of the project are you fundraising for?
When you know what part of the project you need money for you can figure out what fundraising tactic will work best. Some people like to support projects when they can see a tangible result, like a film trailer, while others like the excitement of getting involved at the very beginning and being the first to support a project.

How much time and money do you have to invest in fundraising?
Be honest with yourself about how much time you have to give and how much time you need to raise money. Assess whether the money you can receive from your fundraising campaign is worth the time you will put into it.

Who?

Who are the people most likely to support this project?
Identify the core group of people you expect to support your project. Who are they? Your friends? Your family? Your classmates? Your colleagues? How big is this group and how much money or time do they

have to give? Fundraising starts with your inner circle. These are the people who are already somehow invested in your project and will champion it from the beginning. You need these people to help you spread the word about your fundraising campaign.

Why?
Why should a larger community support this project?
If you are going to be fundraising for a project it needs to be something that has a public benefit, appeals to a charitable impulse, or offers people something they desire. People give because there's something in it for them—whether it be a cool gift, or the connection to an issue they feel passionate about.

Also think about why you are compelled to make the particular project you will be raising money for. What drives you to create what you are making? What are the passions, values, and experiences that you bring to this project? When you raise money you will need to make the case for why the project is important to get people involved in supporting it.

Take time to note responses to each of these questions. When you have concrete answers you are ready to dive into the specifics of your fundraising campaign. There are many ways to raise money, but primarily support for projects either comes from individuals or grant-giving organizations.

Fundraising 101: Raising money from individuals, events, and crowd funding

Individuals make up the most powerful source of philanthropy and charitable giving in the United States. A report by the Giving Institute in 2011 noted that contributions from individuals accounted for 88 percent of philanthropic activity in the United States. What does that mean for you? That building strong relationships with individuals who want to support your project is an effective fundraising strategy.

The majority of individuals who will support your project are people you already know and are connected to: your friends, family, and community. You may be thinking, "But my friends have no money, how can I possibly ask them to support my project?" However, there are many ways to reach people and encourage them to support your project with their hard earned cash. You can start small. Even people who have limited budgets often spend money on things like fancy coffee or craft beer. Perhaps they can give this habit up for a week and donate the amount they would have spent to your project instead. To get people motivated to give to your project you can use fundraising strategies such as: organizing an event, launching an outreach campaign, or running a "crowd funding" campaign, which is using an online platform like Kickstarter to spread the word about your project and collect donations.

When deciding which strategy to use, think about the community you identified as most likely to support your project. What kind of outreach will connect with them and inspire them to give? Fundraising can be a great outlet for your creativity when figuring out the best way to reach this community.

ORGANIZING FUNDRAISING EVENTS

We have all been to a benefit show, dance, dinner, potluck, picnic, auction, or walk-a-thon. These are fundraising events in various guises. Organizing an event helps spread the word about your project, get more community members involved in supporting it, and brings people together in a way that is fun, social, and informative. Before the first Portland Zine Symposium we threw a zinesters's "prom" that made fun of a high school tradition, but also was a creative twist on the traditional benefit show so that more people were motivated to attend and talk about it with their friends. Each holiday season the Desk Set, a librarian social group, holds a benefit bash for the New York City-based organization Literacy for Incarcerated Teens. Not only do they put on a fantastic event that sells out in advance because they have great bands, DJs, performances, and literary themed cocktails, but they motivate people to give more to the cause when their at the event by offering great raffle prizes. They also play upon a strong curiosity factor: because the stereotype of a librarian is someone who is quiet and shy, many people come to the event because they are curious about what a librarian planned party is like (hint: it's a lot of fun). At the same time its fun to plan a party, organizing events is also a lot of work and can be very expensive. Before you decide to throw a fabulous benefit party, think carefully.

Key ideas to consider when organizing a fundraising event:

- What is the incentive that will get people to come out and spend their money?

- Who is your audience?

- Time your fundraiser to an important milestone on the project's timeline

  - Are you launching or wrapping up an important phase of the project?

  - What is the newsworthy item that will make people excited about supporting your project at this time?

- Match the tone of your event to your project. If you are organizing a campaign against police brutality, a carnival style, burlesque fundraiser might not be the strongest fit

- Publicize the event as a fundraiser, not just a fun party, and ensure guests are willing to open up their wallets and hearts to support your cause. There are practical and logistical elements to consider when planning an event:

  - Plan three to six months in advance

  - Make a budget for your event

  - Plan three to six months in adva Secure space, entertainment, and refreshments ake a budget for your event

  - Charge enough for tickets to cover expenses and raise money for your project

  - P ublicize the event and sell tickets in advance

Events are a great opportunity to bring together a community around a DIY project. Enlist others to get involved and to help you organize the event. Shannon Stratton, the Founder and Executive and Creative Director of threewalls gallery in Chicago explains how she engages her core supporters around events, "I get people who care about us, who have a passion for the resource we have created and understand why we matter, to ask others to give to us and get involved."

After the event is over, reflect and analyze what worked well and what you would do differently next time.

GROWING SUPPORT FROM INDIVIDUALS

Reaching out to individuals one-on-one through email, a letter, or in person is a great way to cultivate a relationship and ask them for their financial support. When you reach out you are offering potential supporters compelling reasons to get involved in an exciting, creative project that will effect positive cultural change. Creative people sometimes fear that asking for support and money can be interpreted as an act of desperation, but if you are clear about your project's goals, why the project is important to you, and why support from individuals is needed and appreciated, you can ask with confidence.

The more secure and personal you are, the more likely people will be drawn into your project. For starters, add a personal touch to your communication. For example, Justin Hocking draws a picture or writes a note on every piece of mail that goes to the Independent Publishing Resource Center's dedicated supporters.

When asking individuals for their support:

- Be clear about the project and its goals.
- Explain why now is a transformative time for the project.
- Be positive and upbeat. Do not beg or complain.
- Let them know you need additional support to make the project happen.
- Tell them what is it in for them if they support your project.

- Ask them for a specific amount of money or type of support.

- Be open to questions, dialogue, and negotiation.

- Thank them for their time and consideration, whether they give or not.

Above all, let your passion and dedication show through and be respectful of your potential supporters' time and opinions.

CROWD FUNDING

Crowd funding is a technique of raising money from individuals that has grown in popularity in the past few years by using an Internet platform to mobilize the power of many small individual donations. While Kickstarter, IndieGoGo, and RocketHub are the three best-known platforms, there are many platforms available and new sites with different takes on crowd funding and focused on specific disciplines launch frequently. These platforms use the power of social media to help creative people with a great idea reach out to their friends and fans who then receive an incentive for contributing financially to the project. This model is making the process of raising money more accessible and democratic. It's exciting and still very new, but its popularity is not to be underestimated as Kickstarter and other crowd-funding websites have grown to be a significant source for generating funding for creative projects in the U.S.

Shannon Stratton, Founder and Executive and Creative Director of threewalls gallery in Chicago explains the benefit of having a wide network already in place when you embark on a crowd-funding campaign. "Fundraising is where your network gets really valuable. We did a crowd-funding campaign through Kickstarter for *Phonebook*, a listing of artist run spaces in North America, and raised the money to print it because people who invested in the project felt strongly about the resource existing and we relied on them to tell their friends."

Crowd funding is organized around a campaign model. You fundraise for a specific creative project to get it off the ground or take it to the next level for a determined period of time. First you create an online profile with basic information about you and your project, which can include making a short pitch video. Then, you decide on the amount of money you suggest people give. In most cases, donations to crowd-funding campaigns are not tax deductible, but you instead offer rewards for giving to your project.

Crowd funding enables you to take your social capital and transform it into actual capital you can use to pay for your project. According to Brian Meece, the founder and CEO of the crowd-funding platform RocketHub, successful crowd funding is similar to the "Nineties band model," where you slowly build an audience for your project by reaching out, connecting with dedicated fans and adding value along the way. Crowd funding is not a magic bullet to tap into the money of thousands of donors previously unknown to you. Many artists I have worked with who have not yet run a crowd-funding campaign see it as an "easy" solution to raising money. Crowd funding is not an easy fundraising option, but a more democratic fundraising model that has fewer of the mysterious trappings shrouding grant writing or institutional funding. It can be a great technique that opens up more options when it comes to fundraising for creative projects.

While it may feel like your effort could be similarly spent selling your product instead of running a fundraising campaign, consider that when done properly, crowd-funding can result in media coverage, new fans, and strengthened relationships that will be valuable to your project later.

Before launching your crowd-funding campaign, clarify your fundraising goal, have a catchy description and publicity materials for your project, and ensure you have the time and energy to dedicate to running a campaign.

Core Components of a Successful Crowd funding Campaign

Brian Meece, RocketHub CEO and Co-Founder

Beyond good preparation and planning, these elements will make your fundraising campaign a success:

- Create an exciting project that is worthy of people's attention.

  Potential supporters want to know about you as the artist and your burning desire to make something. Demonstrate how you are infusing your passion into this endeavor and how it is worthy of people's money. Highlight "why" your project matters to you and the world.

- Know your fan-base, audience, and network—they are the ones who will support the project and spread the word to new communities. Identify the community of people who are attached to you and your project. Get them excited about giving and sharing. Crowd-funding success never starts with strangers. Give your existing fans the tools they need and reasons to spread the word.

- Create cool rewards. Give creative rewards in exchange for a financial contribution. Give people the incentive to get involved, and make them feel special. Every award should feel like you are offering something to a person you have a crush on.

Whether you are raising money through events, a crowd-funding campaign, or soliciting for support in other creative ways, individuals are powerful sources of support and getting the work out for your project.

FUNDRAISING 101: RAISING MONEY FROM INSTITUTIONS: GRANTS

Once your project is established, especially if you are starting a nonprofit organization or working on a creative project with a clear social benefit, you may be ready to apply for grants. Grant makers give out money and support to specific projects or organizations that complement their mission. Grants range in size from very small to very large and are the product of building a relationship and entering into a partnership with a funding organization. Every grant is different, though most have an application process that asks you to supply basic information about your project and explain how it fits in with the funder's mission. Getting a grant takes a lot of planning and hard work, but it can bring greater attention, prestige, and resources to your project.

Grants mainly come from two sources: public organizations, such as a state, local, or regional government entities, and private foundations.

Public funders support projects that enhance and add value to a particular community through social programs, arts and culture, education, and research. The money they give out is often from taxpayers, so they have clear incentive to ensure that the projects and people they support benefit a particular community.

Private funders have a specific mission for what they want to achieve in the world and they use their money to give grants to projects that support and enable them to further that mission. Generally foundations only give in certain areas that relate to their mission.

Building relationships with funders works just like building relationships with anyone else.

Here are some basic ground rules for interacting with funders:

- Be polite.

- Thank them for their time and attention.

- Keep your questions succinct and focused.

- Respect the funder's guidelines, process, and timeframe.

- Put yourself in their shoes—ask yourself what the funder wants and what their motivations are for giving out money and support.

The grant process explained
When you decide to seek grants for support of your project give yourself plenty of time. Many funders have specific deadlines and can take several months, and sometimes as long as a year, to get back to you about their decisions.

The grant process happens in three phases:

- Research, or "prospecting" in fundraising speak

- Applying

- Reporting and follow-up

Research

Before you begin your research be very clear what you are fundraising for, what part of your project you are funding and about how much money you will need. This will help you determine if a grant is the right fit for your efforts.

There are several databases that list artist funders, such as the Foundation Center and the Source Database maintained by the New York Foundation for the Arts. Local arts councils and libraries also often maintain information about grants. Search by keywords and within your region. Do not neglect small, local funders such as your local or regional arts council or community foundation, often they will offer smaller size grants to support local projects.

What to look for when researching funders:

- Mission: what do they do and why

- Guidelines: what do you need to apply

- Deadlines: by when do you need to apply

- Past support: who have they given to in the past and how much

- Who is involved in the organization: Who is on their board and staff? Do you know them? Do they care about things that you do? Who is your contact person for questions?

Create a document or a spreadsheet where you can note this information, along with the funders contact information and website, so that it can be easily accessible.

Once you have done your initial research and found funders you are interested in, it is time to determine if they are a good fit for your project. Here are some questions to ask yourself:

- Is my project in one of the areas that they fund? How does my project, and my project's mission statement, line up with their mission?

- Have they funded projects similar to mine in the past?

- How much money do they give out? Is the amount similar to the amount I plan to ask for? What is their time frame? If their deadline is not for three months and your project is happening now, the timing may not be right.

If you have questions you can always contact the person who oversees particular funding programs and can answer questions about it. Many artists I work with are very shy about contacting funders with questions, but if you are concise and polite it can be very helpful for your project. Funders want to receive strong applications because it makes their job easier, so you want to be sure you are getting them what they want, how they want it.

NONPROFIT STATUS AND FISCAL SPONSORSHIP

In the U.S., when researching grants, notice whether the funders you are interested in give to individuals or to organizations with nonprofit status. Nonprofit status is also called 501(c)(3) status, which refers to the part of the U.S. tax code that designates an organization as performing a charitable function. Donors are encouraged to support these charities because they can receive a tax deduction for giving to them. Nonprofit organizations must apply to the IRS for this status. There's information about whether or not to form a nonprofit in "Legal Basics" (see page 82). If you find that most of the grant makers you are interested in require 501(c)(3) status to be eligible, you might consider finding a *fiscal sponsor*.

A fiscal sponsor is an existing nonprofit organization that enables you to use their nonprofit status to collect tax-deductible funds for your project. Fiscal sponsorship can be a great alternative to starting a nonprofit for individuals or small collectives because they save you from the administrative headache, enable you to be eligible for a wider array of grants, and offer individuals a tax-deduction for giving to your project. A fiscal sponsor takes a small percentage of what you raise, often between 5 and 10 percent, in order to cover the administrative cost of handling your donations. A reputable fiscal sponsor will offer you a contract that clearly outlines the terms of your relationship and most only work with projects that are similar in mission to their own. The San Francisco Study Center has more information on fiscal sponsorship and maintains a national directory of fiscal sponsors.

APPLYING FOR GRANTS

Once you have identified the funders that are a good fit for your project, the next step is to apply. Make a calendar with all the grant deadlines you have coming up and start working on your application about a month before the deadline. Each grant application is different and so you must customize your application to what the funder wants. In general, grant applications contain some or all of these elements:

Project narrative
A description of your project that includes project history, mission, goals, and timeline.

Budget
Funders may ask that your budget show both income and expenses. Income can be what you hope to receive, which is called "projected income." Submit you entire project budget, not just what the grant will be used for. This way funders can understand where the money they may give you will fit into the larger project.

Your resume or bio
Highlight accomplishments related to the kind of project you are applying for.

Work samples

For artists this may be examples of your work and for social action projects it may include pictures and descriptions of past projects or events.

Evaluation Plan

This is a plan that tells funders how you will evaluate your project and how you will measure whether or not it was successful. Include specific, measurable, and attainable goals you set for your project and use them as a basis to create a plan to measure what worked and what could be improved for your project.

If you are applying for several grants it's a good idea to keep generic versions of your application materials on file and customize them to each funding opportunity.

Overall, when applying for grants remember to:

- Read the guidelines carefully

- Ensure you have answered each question

- Write in clear, straightforward prose

- Proofread your application

- Submit your application by the deadline

Following the funder's guidelines and directions and presenting your project clearly will make your application stand out from the crowd.

Grant reporting and follow up

Once you have submitted your application the most you can do is wait. It never hurts to send an email or call the funder to ensure that they received your application and to ask when you can expect a response.

When you hear back from the foundation your proposal will either be accepted or rejected.

If you are accepted:

- Thank them immediately for their time, consideration, and generosity.

- Notify your mailing list and any collaborators about the good news.

- Ask the funder how they expect you to report on the grant.

- Ensure that you gather documentation, such as statistics, quotes, testimonials, and photographs, needed for the reports.

- Ask the funder how they would like to be publicly acknowledged.

- Keep in touch with the funder and ensure they are up-to-date on your project's activities.

If you are declined:

- Acknowledge the funder's time and consideration: Even if you were not accepted your proposal was still reviewed by a panel of experts.

- Ask for feedback to strengthen your future proposals.

- Ask about reapplying and if you are eligible.

- Remain professional and positive in your interactions with funders. It can be frustrating to be rejected, but work to not take it personally.

Grant writing is a skill that takes time to develop. I work with many artists who get frustrated about the time it takes to prepare grant applications, the amount of detail they need to provide about their project, and the fact that many grants are very competitive and difficult to win. If you are applying to a lot of grants, form a fundraising support group to keep motivated. Get together regularly with friends and allies to give each other feedback on each other's fundraising ideas, celebrate your successes and vent your frustration. Grants are only one way to raise money. Work to balance your fundraising strategy between earned income, in-kind support, individual donations, events, and crowd funding. Push yourself to be creative to find the resources you need for your project.

BUILD A HEALTHY RELATIONSHIP WITH MONEY

The financial side of your project supports the creative side and tells the full story of what you are working to achieve. When you raise money to support your project, whether from grants, individuals, crowd funding, or events, you build relationships. Keep track of and keep in touch with those who support you. Shannon Stratton of threewalls gallery suggests, "Hold events for your supporters where you are not expecting anything out of them. When you acknowledge peoples' support it makes everyone feel like they matter." Justin Hocking of the Independent Publishing Resource Center agrees, "Be organized so you don't have to keep all of your fundraising information in your head because it crowds out the creativity. When you keep track of and acknowledge details about donors it inspires connections with people and community." Showing good will towards your supporters' generosity is a sure strategy for building long lasting relationships of support.

To keep in touch with the people who have supported me, whether freelance clients, friends who have leant a hand to my projects, or professional colleagues from past full-time jobs, I always send a handmade, hand written card around the New Year. It's a great way to keep in touch and let people know I am thinking of them and appreciate them. Because this small gesture of recognition is tied to an annual celebration I also remember to do it and because it is creative, I look forward to creating it.

When you have a clear vision of your finances you have a clear vision for your project. A plan for what resources you need to make your project happen and how you will find those resources makes your project strong. Tim Haft of Punk Rope emphasizes the importance of financial planning connected to general project planning,

For me, rethinking my relationship to money and finance has helped me know what is realistic for me to achieve creatively. I've become wiser about the creative choices I make. I feel more confident about the outside projects I take on because I know they will benefit and strengthen my creative practice. For example, I was offered a part-time job for a company whose mission I wholeheartedly supported, but I realized that the money I would make was not worth the time I would give up working on my own projects.

Once I developed a clear idea of my personal and project related expenses I have been better able to decide when to move certain creative projects forward and when to wait until I had resources available to take the next step.

Thinking about money and finances can be intimidating at first, but once you have a plan and a budget you can make the money work for you.

As filmmaker William E. Badgley said, "Thinking about money won't crush your project. It will strengthen it."

> *"If you can't pay your bills you can't do what you want. Have fun, share what you do, but have a plan to keep yourself from wandering aimlessly without a map."*
>
> *-Tim Haft*

CHAPTER 2 CHECKLIST:

- Financial empowerment is creative empowerment

- Create a financial plan to enable your project to grow sustainably

- Tell the story of your project in numbers by making a budget

- Track your expenses and revisit your budget often

- Price your work enough to make it worth it and pay yourself fairly

- Do not forget about taxes—as independent as you are, you are obligated to pay them

- Talk to an accountant if necessary

- Match your fundraising strategy to the kind of project you are creating

- Thank and keep in touch with your supporters regularly

CHAPTER 3

BUILDING COMMUNITY AND SPREADING THE WORD: DO IT YOURSELF

MARKETING, IDENTITY, AND MEDIA

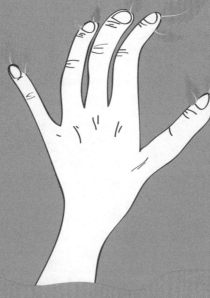

Your project needs other people to see it, read it, hear it, enjoy it, and respond to it in order to be successful. In addition to empowering yourself to create your vision, a do it yourself project also builds community between individuals.

Let's think about ways to spread the word about your project in person, in print, and online. You'll need to identify the specific audience for your project and form a strategy to reach them. You know your project from the inside out, but now it's time to take a step back and think about how the outside world sees it. We will talk about how you can form an "identity" for your project that people can relate to that encompasses who you are and what your project is all about. We'll also cover how to develop a catchy pitch for your project, and craft that pitch into an outreach and marketing strategy. Outreach builds specific relationships with allies for your project for collaboration and promotion. While you might feel like "marketing" is only for corporations and has nothing to do with your project, it is really about crafting a focused message about who you are and what you make. Once you've honed that message that you can spread the word about what you do through your online presence, on social media, and by building relationships with journalists, bloggers, and other media members to broadcast your message to a larger public.

When you launch an outreach and publicity campaign you want to help your audience think about your project in a meaningful way and understand how it connects to their life. Before launching a media campaign, ensure that your project is strong and ready for the world to see it. You are informing the public about why they should care, and what's in it for them if they get involved. You want to have something with substance for your audience to latch on to.

Your outreach and marketing strategy can be as unique as you and your project.

When crafting this strategy revisit your project's mission goals. The "identity" you create for your project and outreach you undertake should reflect these goals.

The feedback you receive from pushing your project to a larger audience will help you refine your ideas and make them stronger. Antonio Ramos of Brooklyn Soda Works advised, "Learn your market. You have to find out how much people like what you are making. Customer's collective behavior and response is invaluable to making your product better. Let their feedback drive your decisions."

MARKET RESEARCH: WHO NEEDS YOUR PROJECT?

Amy Cuevas Schroeder, founder of the DIY Business Association, said, "It takes a community to do it yourself." Figure out what kind of support you need from other people to make your project a success. These people could be customers, volunteers, audience, or collective members. When you define who they are you can determine how to reach them.

Questions to ask about your project:

- Are you selling a product that needs customers?

- Are you performing or presenting and need audience members?

- Are you building a public movement or campaign and need volunteers and public supporters?

- Are you taking on a large-scale project where you will need partners, collaborators, or collective members?

Revisit your brainstorm from chapter one when you identified the target market or community for your project. Who is already connected to your project? You may already be making a zine, playing in a band, or working with a collective. Does the audience that you imagine for your project resemble this group of people or will you need to expand who you reach in order to achieve the success you dream of?

To reach the audience of your dreams think of specific people who you would like to know about your project. These people are your "target market." Next find out how they are getting information about new products, projects, services, and events. Do they find out through social media? From friends? Is there a certain print or online publication or newsletter they read? How do you find information and new things that are of interest to you? What motivates you to try something new?

When identifying a target market for your project, think outside your immediate community. What other organizations and networks of people are interested in the ideas and issues that drive your project? For example, for their Dinner and Bikes tour, bicycle advocate and writer Elly Blue, filmmaker (and publisher of this book) Joe Biel, and vegan chef Joshua Ploeg, reached out to bicycle transit advocacy groups to set up their events. They found that at least every major city had a group like this one and that they had strong, established networks that were excited about a creative presentation and discussion of relevant issues. By reaching out to this group they were able to find new audiences for their work that reached beyond the punk, bike, and vegan underground culture that they had reached on previous tours.

Once you have a clear idea of who it is you want to reach, devise a strategy to reach them that can include networking and personal outreach, web, social media presence, and media outreach.

IDENTIFY YOURSELF

Before you launch a major outreach campaign you need to know who you are. While I've chosen to focus on creating an identity for my project, identity creation can also be considered "branding." While "branding" conjures up slick images of expensive advertising firms, the idea of branding does not belong to corporations alone. When you create an identity for your project you are empowering yourself to take control of your image. You choose to send a consistent message that determines how the wider world sees you and understands what you do. How do you want to be known?

Think about your favorite independent projects. How do they identify themselves? Do they have a logo that's easily recognizable? A tag line that immediately let's you know their core values? Do you trust them to be consistent in what they put out? For example, Dischord Records from Washington DC has identified themselves as a politically astute label that's fiercely independent, musically interesting, and active in the punk

What do you want to be known for? You decide!

scene. The website Etsy has build their reputation as a great resource to find handmade goods, and identified themselves as a supportive community for crafters. *Bust* magazine's tag line is the magazine for "women with something to get off their chests," and they have positioned themselves as smart, stylish, crafty, feminist, and fun. The band the Shondes, who you will read more about later in this chapter, have created a strong identity for themselves as a high-energy, independent, queer, feminist, rock band. They embrace their Jewish heritage and tradition, but are politically pro-Palestinian, so those who go to their shows know they are going to have a politically and artistically engaged experience.

Before you release your project to the world, define an identity for it. Like creating a mission statement, crafting a public identity for your project takes time and careful consideration. Your project may develop overtime, but its overall identity should stay consistent. For example, I've been publishing my personal zine *Indulgence* for over 15 years. While my writing has developed and the specific content of the writing changed, when readers pick up the zine they trust they will read thoughtfully written, politically engaged, personal essays in a creatively designed, handmade package.

Quick tips for creating an identity for your project:

- Explain your project in one sentence. Be focused and concise

- What are 5 key words you want associated with your project?

- What personality do you want associated with your project?

- How will the personality of your project be represented visually?

- What is the reputation you want to build?

- How will your project stand out from similar ones?

- Keep your project's identity consistent across mediums, whether its web, print, or in-person

When you are developing your project's identity, define how it is different, new, and exciting. If the people you want to reach are already engaged with similar projects, what about yours will make them want to get involved?

DEVELOP YOUR PITCH

When you introduce your project to someone new you "pitch" it to him or her as something exciting and positive that they need to know about. It's helpful to have a pitch prepared that is a concise, memorable statement about your project that easily rolls off your tongue. To develop your pitch revisit your project's goals and mission statement. They can easily be crafted into your pitch for outreach. You will use this pitch in your printed and online materials, press releases, emails, and calls to people you want to collaborate with, as well as in casual conversation.

Your pitch should include:

- The who, what, where, when, and why of your project

- A catchy, memorable description, or "tag-line" for your project

- Basic information about who you are

Your pitch should reflect the identity, personality, and message that you have decided on for your project. Is it friendly and welcoming? Avant-garde and intriguing? Ensure that it is consistent with the image you want to reflect.

Greta Gertler, Musician and head of Goldfish Prize PR, emphasizes the personal behind the pitch, "The story of what you are doing is important. It is not just that your project is really great, but that you are sharing a story behind it. People are bombarded with inputs and you want your story to stand out."

Write down your pitch in a paragraph and then shorten it to a sentence. That one sentence is sometimes known as your "elevator pitch"—if you were in an elevator with someone and you had 30 seconds to tell them about what you are working on, what would you say? Will you ask a question or share a fact to intrigue and involve your audience? Write it down and practice saying it out loud. Share it with friends for feedback.

CULTIVATING PERSONAL CONNECTIONS THROUGH OUTREACH

Networking is the basis of the do it yourself community and what makes the DIY community so special. It also is an important strategy for spreading the word about your project that goes deeper than traditional marketing. When you develop an outreach strategy you identify organizations or individuals who could have a special interest in your project and reach out to them on a one-on-one basis before you launch a large-scale marketing campaign.

First, define and identify whom you would like to connect with about your project. Are there other creative people or organizations you want to collaborate with? Could they share advice with you? Perhaps you are trying to reach the same group of people and you could combine your efforts? Maybe you want to ensure that, as a newcomer, you are not stepping on their toes and will reach out to be polite.

Personal connections are very important to your project's success. When I was co-publishing *riffRAG*, an art journal focused on emerging, queer, and feminist artists, before we released an open call for submissions we reached out directly to artists we knew and admired that we wanted to include in the magazine. That way we knew we would already have a strong base of contributors who were excited and invested in the project and whose work would be a great fit for the publication. In addition, because those artists were excited to be included and felt personally connected to us they were motivated to help spread the word about the call for submissions and to support the magazine when it came out.

Successful outreach requires reaching the right person, especially in the case of an organization. Once you have identified who that person is, pick up the phone or write a concise, polite, personal email.

Key elements to an engaging outreach conversation:

- Introduce yourself

- Summarize your project (use your pitch!)

- Explain why you are contacting them and propose how you could work together

- Give them a reason to work with you

- Invite them to discuss further or to ask questions

- Thank them for their time and consideration

If you don't hear back right away, follow up after a week. People are busy, but it helps to be persistent without bombarding them with communication.

Community building is key when conducting outreach. Outreach opens communication and offers you a chance to receive feedback and exchange ideas with those with whom you contact. Just like any kind of communication, confidence in your project and what you are offering is important to successful outreach. When I am reaching out to editors to pitch freelance articles or clubs to book my band I always remind myself that I have something important to offer them—great content—in exchange for new opportunities. When you approach outreach communication with a positive, confident attitude you develop relationships with peers, supporters, and advocates who can support you throughout the life of your project.

YOUR PRESENCE ON THE WEB

A website is your opportunity to share all the information your audience needs to understand you and your project. You need to create your website before you begin major outreach because those curious about your project need to have a place to go to find out more about it. It need not be fancy, but should clearly reflect the identity you have chosen for your project, highlight your name and the name of your project, and include basic information about you and how to contact you.

Basic tips for your website:

- Have one

- Keep navigation as simple as possible

- Use readable fonts and high contrast colors

- Include basic information about your project such as: description, your bio or resume, upcoming events, how to order goods you have for sale, contact information

- Link to your website on social media

- Ensure your website loads and reads easily on multiple browsers and operating systems

- Tag your site with key words so that it comes up in searches. Do a test search using these terms to see if your site comes up in top five results. Keep tweaking key words until it does

- Keep information up-to-date

A good, clean functional website can be affordable. There are many free website and blog services that offer templates that you can plug in your information to and customize further. Others offer template websites for specific disciplines, such as visual artists, or musicians.

Before committing to a specific service spend some time looking at the sites they host. Evaluate your site building options:

- Do you like the overall look and functionality?

- Do they offer what you need?

- Can you update it easily?

- Does the platform use open source software and are they committed to staying on the cutting edge of technology?

- Identify a platform you can grow with.

Be active on social media

Online communities are real communities and social media gives you the tools you need to engage with them. While a website provides basic information about your project, social media adds a personal touch to your web presence. It is an opportunity for your audience to get a behind the scenes look at your project and get to know you better. Building community using social media is a great way to connect with people who share your interests and can support your project no matter where they live.

For me as a zine maker and reader who has traded zines with and wrote letters to similar-minded self-publishers all over the world, social media feels like a similar kind of conversation, just sped-up and available in real time. It's important to be personable, authentic, and honest on social media because relationships forged online are still relationships.

As I've shifted from writing a zine to blogging I've found the process of building a community through like-minded bloggers to be similar to that of zine makers. The international community of bloggers I've been able to forge do share my interests: they focus on personal life, feminism, food, and fashion, and we can "chat" constantly on Twitter and through blog commentary. It's a great feeling to have an insight into what someone in another culture, time zone, or country is doing, thinking, and responding to. I feel this kind of interaction and connection enriches my life and brings a greater perspective to my projects.

Social media can be very accessible if you think of it as a worldwide conversation that is evolving constantly. Social media offers you a fantastic opportunity to join that conversation. It can be tempting to be snarky and off-handed on the Internet, but be careful, because it is very hard, if not impossible, to erase something you regret saying. Post as if everything you say will be archived and searchable in the future. You don't want your present or future reputation haunted by your Internet past.

The world of social media changes fast and new platforms and ideas for information sharing are launching constantly. For those new to social media, or who are familiar only with a few sites, it can feel overwhelming to take on yet another platform. Develop a social media strategy to help you decide on which platforms to engage and how you can use social media to best spread the word about your project.

SOCIAL MEDIA GUIDELINES

- Choose the platform(s) that you will update and feel comfortable using

- Research which platforms your audience is using and be active on those

- Update regularly

- Ensure that your posts on social media are consistent with the identity you have created for your project

- Respond to and interact with others

- Promote others' projects and share information in addition to promoting yourself

- Know the popular social media influencers in your field

As you develop your voice and presence on social media stay on top of the trends and new developments in technology, even if you do not consider yourself a techie. As a creative person in any medium your audience will look to you for advice and indication about what's new and cool. Be informed about the next big thing, even if you don't choose to use it. Connect your reasons for choosing one platform over another to your identity and the goals of your project.

Build your audience using blogs and social media

An interview with Stephanie Rousseau, Art Director, Illustrator, and author of the fashion and design blog *By Glam*

How is the content on your blog and your presence on social media related to your freelance work as a designer, illustrator, and art director?
It's a great window for my work. It allows me to build my reputation and find new clients. My blog, social media presence, and freelance business are all linked, so I approach everything with the same energy and always try to improve the quality of what I create.

How did you find, connect with, and grow the audience for your blog?
It is important for me to do a "good job" and present high quality photos, nice illustrations, and accomplished graphic design. I am constantly looking at the "best" blogs in order to adjust the design and functionality of mine to be better for my readers.

How do you identify the platforms that resonate for you and are useful for your projects?
I'm a little crazy about social media platforms and every time I hear about a new one I sign up! After that I take my time to see if I need to be on that platform or not.

How do you ensure that your "message" and personality on each platform remains consistent?
I try to offer different content on each platform, but it takes a lot of time! The most difficult part is to give a part of you, but don't give everything away. You must be careful: be genuine, but don't reveal private information.

What do you advise for developing an active, effective social media strategy?
Be yourself! Social media personality is really important! I want to give [this additional content] to my readers. Be careful of "following" too many people because they will get lost in your timeline. It is polite to interact with the people you follow. If you update your blog and your social media platforms frequently, readers will come often to see what is new and subscribe to your feed.

BEST PRACTICES: SELLING HANDMADE ITEMS AND BUILDING COMMUNITY ONLINE

From Danielle Maveal, Founder of Creative Little Beasts website and podcast, Oh My! Handmade, and former head of Seller Education at Etsy

Selling DIY goods online is an extension of the community that you build and the presence that you create. Below are ideas on how to focus your web presence on generating interest in your e-shop.

Focus on what you are selling:

- Spend time and money on product development

- Create a focused line of work

- Value your unique point of view

- Develop a strong, consistent brand

- Cultivate hardcore fans by appealing to a smaller, more passionate market

Romance the buyer by spending time on the writing and visuals of your profile or site:

- Speak from your perspective about your process and inspiration

- What kind of person would love what you are selling?

Put enough work out online so that potential buyers will notice you:

- Have a blog, put new items in your shop, make good use of visual social networks, like Pinterest or Flickr

- Stick with it—your audience doesn't arrive quickly

Value your creative community as a resource:

- Know when you are in over your head

- Reach out to others for support and motivation: Create a team on Etsy or other creative community website(s) or find a local group that fits your needs and the vibe you want

- Identify a mentor to work with to learn from their experience and perspective

- Be consistent, flexible, learn from your mistakes and keep going

PRESS OUTREACH: ENGAGING TRADITIONAL MEDIA

When your project is complete, you cross a newsworthy milestone, or you are ready to reach a wider audience, you can reach out to the news media to gain a wider following and publicize your event.

Similar to fundraising and outreach, building press contacts is about building relationships with prominent bloggers, journalists, and editors. It is up to you to demonstrate for them how your project matches the need of their publication, site, or program.

Start by defining your goals for press coverage. Do you have a publication or album you would like reviewed? Do you want to appear as an "expert guest" on programs or blogs? Do you want to reach a certain community?

Once you are clear on your goals, identify publications, blogs, radio shows, and television programs that cover projects and events similar to yours. Greta Gertler, of Goldfish Prize PR, discusses how she identifies and prioritizes publications to reach out to, "I follow artists that are getting press and who are similar to the ones I am promoting. I see where they are getting written up and target that press."

After you've identified media outlets that are a good fit for your project, look on each website's "about" page or in the publication's masthead. Find editors that work on sections where you are interested in getting coverage. Pitch your idea to them. Publication staff email addresses often follow a formula and you can crack the code to figure out the right person's email address. You can also find relevant people and their contact information in listings like the one Media Bistro puts out.

PLANNING A PRESS CAMPAIGN

From Greta Gertler, musician in the Universal Thump and head of Goldfish Prize PR

When setting up a publicity campaign for a musician or myself, these are the steps that I go through:

- Distribution. How will the final product be distributed? Do they have a label or are they doing it themselves?

- Book a release event. Where will it be?

- Decide on the regions where you want to promote the project and prioritize outreach there.

- Create a tailored list of publications and news outlets that reflects the artist's priorities.

- Craft a newsworthy story about the artist. What angle do they feel comfortable pushing to the media?

- Keep the campaign focused on the project as much as possible.

- Media is personality driven. Craft the campaign based on the personality of the creator and how that supports their project.

- Develop content beyond the project, such as videos, a Facebook page, an active Twitter account, a blog, or photo sharing.

Prioritize your press outreach list. Start with local or niche outlets that are more likely to give you coverage. Pitching smaller, friendlier outlets will help you build confidence and relationships and give you a better understanding of what editors and journalists need from you.

Marisha Chinsky, a musician and PR agent, recommends getting advice from friends and colleagues who have gone through a similar process to your own. *"Hold an informal focus group with community members who are familiar with or passionate about the realm of your project,"* she suggests, *"If you're starting an art gallery, tap into your artist contacts to ask where they go to for art news. If you're opening a yoga studio, ask another local yoga studio and their patrons if they have sources of information in the media. Advice is free, people are keen to help, and communities are supportive if you're friendly and respectful of people's time and opinions."*

Create a calendar of deadlines for submissions and pitches for the publications you are interested in. Many publications work four to six months in advance, if not more, so in order to get timely coverage you may need to pitch much earlier than you think.

Marisha Chinsky also shared advice about how to craft your pitch to editors; "Press releases are less relevant than in the past. With social media, plus the 24/7 news cycle that reporters must keep up a concise, punchy pitch email is more effective than a wordy press release."

She advises to tailor further pitches, for example, "It's worthwhile to connect your pitch to a news hook like a new product launch, store opening, a milestone like your 1,000th customer, or something about your product or service that's connected to a holiday or public event. Maybe you're selling your artisanal soda at the local county fair? Or offering discounts on Halloween?"

Temim Fruchter, who was the drummer for the feminist, independent rock band The Shondes for eight years, handled the band's press and public relations for the past five years and gotten them featured in national magazines such as *Entertainment Weekly* and *Curve*. She shared a set of guidelines for interacting with the media, some of which she has learned through experience the hard way.

PRESS OUTREACH GUIDELINES

Temim Fruchter, drummer for The Shondes

- Know your audience when you are talking to editors and journalists and understand the goals of their publication.

- Cultivate genuine, personal relationships with journalists and editors.

- Edit press releases to fit the publication you are pitching to.

- Provide catchy subject lines and newsworthy items.

- Be short, polite, and persistent in your communication—follow up!

- Meet people in person to discuss opportunities and collaboration

- Network and be open to opportunities of all kinds.

- When meeting journalists always have a story to tell.

- Research other projects at your level who are doing their own press outreach. Where are they getting written up? Network with them and share ideas and tips.

Temim also developed a set of tools that she used to keep a record of contacts and to be efficient in her press outreach, since she often handled press while the band was on tour, recording, or booking shows.

TOOLS FOR EFFECTIVE PRESS OUTREACH

From Temim Fruchter

- Keep and update a spreadsheet or database of media contacts that is searchable, sortable, and well organized.

- Find samples of good press release copy. Revise your press release often and get feedback from people who receive press releases about what works and what doesn't.

- Create press outreach email templates that you can copy, paste, and customize.

- Always include the basic who, what, where, when, why, and how of your project, links to your website, and your contact information in your press materials.

- Have a press resource on your website. Make a one-stop place where people can get catchy quotes, downloadable photos, and basic information about you.

- Make a calendar of publication deadlines for sending out pitches and press releases.

Make images of your project available and easy to access for editors and journalists. Ensure that you have high-quality images sized for web and print publications. Your images should reflect the identity you have created for your project—you don't want to leave an editor scouring the Internet for images of you. I experienced this problem first hand when I was working for a major New York City museum. We presented local bands and performing artists groups and were often the first major venue where they got to perform for a large audience. So few of these performers had press images that were the quality and size we needed to publish that the artists we featured in our advertising were often those who gave us good images, not necessarily the most established artists. As a result, those with nice press images were able to get increased exposure.

Once you begin receiving media attention, keep a record of your press clips, put your press coverage out on your social media and feature clips of and links to coverage on your website. Use your past press coverage to leverage coverage in other outlets. Keep in touch with journalists and editors and keep track of where they work. The media world is small, people move around a lot and they work for a variety of publications. Keep on top of this so that you don't lose a good contact!

CONCLUSION: MARKETING IS COMMUNITY BUILDING

The community I have built over the past 15 years has been vital to supporting my projects as I grow and change. My contacts have become friends, professional mentors, and supporters, and many have known me as my projects shifted from DIY cassettes and records, to handmade zines, to large scale community events, to writing for digital and print publications. Because my projects have always been creative and my approach to them and the community around them was always honest, reliable, and communicative, I've been able to retain and grow my network of support over the years. As a result I have a community around me I can immediately access to help promote and spread the word about new projects that I take on.

Overall, creating an identity for and marketing your project enables you to decide how news about your project reaches a wider audience. Marketing and outreach builds and strengthens the community around your project. When you craft a consistent message and personality that supports your project's mission and goals, you can build community and promote your project at every phase. Reaching out through personal contacts, the web, social media, and traditional media outlets connects you with the wider audience and bigger platforms you need to make your project a success.

CHAPTER 3 SUMMARY AND TIPS

- Identify your community and your market

  o Who is already connected to your project?

  o Who is doing something similar that you would like to be connected to?

  o Identify the leaders in your field. Who do you look to for inspiration?

  o Who will buy your product, use your services, or join your organization?

  o Think about your market demographically—where do they live, how old are they, what do they do for work and fun, how much money do they make?

- Define your project's identity and your pitch

  - What is the personality and reputation you want to show to the world?

  - Craft your "elevator pitch." In one sentence: I am doing___

  - Devise a strategy for Internet presence and media outreach

  - Target specific publications and websites that reflect your project's goals

  - Fit your strategy into your overall project timeline

CHAPTER 4

DIY BUSINESS SENSE: WHAT YOU NEED TO KNOW TO GROW

Having your own business is an opportunity to take charge and support your vision and your life on your own terms. Your project can be as creative, subversive, or as radical as you are and you should build a framework to support that.

It's time to think about basic business structures, terminology, and resources you need to build a strong legal and logistical foundation for your project. We'll talk about the basics of when and how to register as a business, introduce basic business structures, and go over the basics of how to protect yourself and your project with contracts, insurance, and copyright.

There are some basic steps to creating a business that this chapter will cover in more detail. They are:

- Choose a business entity

- Incorporate

- Get a business license

- Obtain the necessary insurance and permits

- Write and sign contracts and memorandums of understanding with your collaborators

While thinking about a business structure can seem overwhelming, it can be more complicated and expensive to sort out your legal needs down the road. Empower yourself, be proactive, and ensure that when you involve the law and government in your project it is on your own terms. Having a legal structure for your business and formalizing your agreements with those you collaborate with will protect you, your project and your creativity.

Registering as a business ensures you have proper structures set up for record keeping, taxation, and governance. As you set goals and a timeline for your project, make registering as a business part of your overall plan if it's applicable to your project.

STARTING A HANDMADE BUSINESS: BROOKLYN SODA WORKS

Brooklyn Soda Works creates artisanal carbonated juices using all natural ingredients and unusual flavor combinations. Founded in 2009 by artist Caroline Mak and chemist Antonio Ramos, the company is a vital part of Brooklyn's growing independent food entrepreneur scene. They sell sodas with flavors like Grapefruit Tarragon or Sassafras and Wintergreen at events around the city and have sodas on tap at local bars. Brooklyn Soda Works began in a friend's restaurant kitchen and they raised their initial capital through a crowd funding campaign. After several years they have grown into their own space in an industrial building in Brooklyn, quit their day jobs, and hired employees. Starting a food business brings a unique set of challenges and opportunities that Antonio and Caroline work to tackle as they appear.

QUESTIONS TO ASK WHEN STARTING A HANDMADE BUSINESS

Caroline Mak and Antonio Ramos of Brooklyn Soda Works

- Why do you want to make this?

- Is there a demand for your product? If you are not sure people want what you are selling, why burden yourself with the work?

- What are your basic costs? What equipment do you need?

- Do you want to move beyond startup and be a sustainable small business?

- How can you scale up? Can you maintain your quality as you make more of your product?

- As you scale up, what aspect of your product do you like and want to keep? Is the hand-madeness essential? If so, price your product accordingly.

SETTING UP YOUR BUSINESS

Create a business structure that will strengthen your project. Caroline Mak, of Brooklyn Soda Works, a Limited Liability Corporation (LLC), explained that she and her partner Antonio Ramos wanted to lay the groundwork for a successful business from the beginning. One of the first steps they took was to register as an LLC.

> *"Figure out your business structure first and incorporate to protect your own assets. For food related businesses know your state's health code and ensure you meet it. Creating an LLC was a straightforward process that we did without a lawyer."*
> *-Caroline Mak*

Shannon Stratton, Founder, Executive and Creative Director of threewalls gallery in Chicago, was similarly clear, "When we decided to start threewalls we were strict about making it a stable organization, so we incorporated immediately as a nonprofit and got our 501(c)(3) status. That was seven months before we opened so that we could focus on fundraising and have all the structures in place to receive money."

Launching a business, or turning your do it yourself project into a legal business, is your ticket to participate in the economy in a way that works for you. There are many resources available for you when you decide to go and grow the do it yourself route. You may not have thought of yourself this way before, but you are walking the path of an entrepreneur when you decide to make a living off your own creativity, ideas, and hard work.

Two important resources are:

SCORE, a nonprofit organization dedicated to the education, support, and growth of fledgling small businesses. They offer free counseling and workshops for start-up businesses all across the country and have a wealth of templates and worksheets available online, including a guide to choosing a legal entity for your business.

THE SMALL BUSINESS ADMINISTRATION (SBA) offers a host of well organized, clearly presented business resources, and discusses considerations for starting eco-friendly businesses, women, and minority owned businesses, self-employed individuals, start ups with high growth potential, nonprofit organizations, and businesses run by people with disabilities. The SBA also includes guides and links to forms for how to incorporate.

SMALL BUSINESS LESSONS FROM PUNK ROPE

Created by Tim Haft and Shana Brady, Punk Rope is an innovative exercise class that combines jump rope skills and conditioning with the fun of recess and the attitude of punk rock. Tim and Shana believe in play as a way to help get people fit and have built their business in a grassroots manner, training other Punk Rope instructors and ambassadors to bring the class to their communities. They shared some pointers around the legal and financial side of building a small business, some of which they learned the hard way.

- Position yourself in such a way that you benefit the most financially from your idea and passion—do not exploit yourself.

- Be protective of your intellectual property and do not give it away outright.

- Protect the business you have created through incorporation and trademark.

- Understand which financial and lifestyle sacrifices you are willing to make for your business and for how long.

- When you start small and have limited financial resources utilize your social capital through barter.

- Leverage media attention, reviews, and mentions into long-term support. Media attention is powerful, though it does not always translate into dollars.

- Have an efficient and strategic presence on social media. Interact with peers and treat it as a "You scratch my back, I'll scratch yours" situation.

- Your initial customers will come from your immediate community. Feel like you are needed within that community. That sense of importance will drive your business.

TIPS FOR DECIDING ON A BUSINESS ENTITY

When you know where you stand legally you can create the groundwork for a sustainable project. Antonio Ramos of Brooklyn Soda Works said, "Put your project first and find a legal structure for your business supports that you want to make."

- Assess how each option for incorporations aligns with your project's goals, vision, and mission.

- Reach out to others with businesses similar to yours and ask them why they chose the entity they did and what their experience has been.

- Choose your business entity carefully—changing it later can create a legal headache.

- If you're incorporating with the help of a lawyer know what you need from them and what you can do yourself.

Ramos also advises, "For business, accounting and legal help: try doing something yourself first, before talking to a professional. That way you understand how you personally keep track of money or understand laws and can ask better questions. You can get the best deal possible when you understand the specific problems and questions you have."

TYPES OF BUSINESS

In the U.S. there are several major types of business entities. Research what is available to you in your state. The Small Business administration lists links and information on incorporating state by state. Depending on what state you are incorporating in some forms may be legal and others may not be. In addition, the process of incorporation works slightly differently depending where you live. I've talked with many creative people who have great business ideas, but are intimidated by the incorporation process and question whether it is necessary. If you are serious about creating and growing a successful, sustainable business, take the time to incorporate so that you can provide your business with the foundation it needs to grow.

Below are the basic entities:

SOLE PROPRIETORSHIP: The most common business entity for a DIY or freelance project. Sole proprietorship gives you complete control and is easy to set up because your business is simply you. However, it does not limit your liability, meaning that your company's liability is your own personal liability. The same goes for taxes—you file taxes for both your personal earnings and the business. However both of these details may be moot if you do not have personal assets to protect in the first place. If you don't own property or have a significant amount of money, liability may not be an issue.

      If your business has a name other than your own you will need to file a "Doing Business As" or "DBA" with your county clerk for your new or "fictitious" business name. The Small Business Administration has a chart on their website that lists the requirements for registering your DBA in each state.

PARTNERSHIP: Many DIY projects are joint ventures, meaning that you are working on them with someone else. If you are starting a business with two or more people who are contributing money, property, and expertise, you could consider forming a partnership. There are several different types of partnerships with different requirements for taxation, liability, and legal responsibility. Partners often have to pay taxes on the businesses profits and their personal profits, which can be very high. In addition, you want to ensure you have a legal agreement with your business partner that clearly outlines each of your responsibility(s) and liability(s), should any problems arise later.

COOPERATIVE: These nonprofit businesses are owned and managed by the people who use their services, work, or live there. They have a history in Britain and America of dedication to the empowerment of working people. Think about your local food or childcare co-op as an example. Co-ops are a democratic structure that requires you create bylaws, a membership application for voting members, and have a board of directors that govern the co-op. The National Co-Op Business Association has established seven co-op principles and provides information about how to start a co-op.

CORPORATION: One of the oldest business structures in the United States, a corporation is a legal entity that is independent from its founders and is owned by its shareholders and governed by a board of directors. The corporation, and not its shareholders, is held legally liable for its taxes, profits, and debts. For a perspective on the implications of this structure at the larger level, the 2004 film *The Corporation* by Mark Achbar, Jennifer Abbott and Joel Bakan is required watching. Depending on the type of corporation you form, such as a C-Corporation or S-Corporation, your business will pay taxes on an annual or quarterly schedule and you will have different tax obligations. Overall, corporations are the most expensive and complicated business entity to form.

LIMITED LIABILITY CORPORATION (LLC): A hybrid-legal structure that offers flexibility like a partnership, but protects the partners from liability like a corporation. LLCs can be owned by one or more people, and taxes are passed on to the owners of the LLC. Many filmmakers will create an LLC for their film to protect themselves from liability on their film shoots. The process of forming an LLC varies from state-to-state and LLCs are not legal in all states.

SOCIAL BENEFIT CORPORATION (B CORPORATION): A relatively new corporate structure that values people, the planet, and profit, B Corps aim to address the gap between for-profit and nonprofit legal entities. They use for-profit models to address social and environmental issues. B Corps are certified by a nonprofit organization, B Lab, as adhering to certain environmental, labor, and social benefit standards and are not yet legal in all states. To create a B Corp you must first incorporate using one of the structures above and then apply to B Lab for certification.

NONPROFIT: Many DIY projects that are based in social activism or provide a community service consider forming a nonprofit to make their work more sustainable and longer lasting. These organizations provide a public benefit and service and use their profits to improve their services. Because they are serving a charitable purpose they are exempt from taxation, but still must file reports on their annual financial activities with the IRS. Forming a nonprofit is a two-step process. First you must incorporate on the state level and then apply to the IRS for your federal, tax-exempt status. This status, the most common of which is called 501(c)(3) in the tax-code, enables individuals to receive a tax-deduction for giving to your organization and makes your nonprofit eligible for many grant programs. If you are considering forming a nonprofit you might consider working with a fiscal sponsor first before incorporating on you own. See page 48 for more information about fiscal sponsorship.

PROFILE: THREEWALLS GALLERY: BUILDING A SMALL, SUSTAINABLE CREATIVE NONPROFIT

Shannon Stratton, Founder, Executive and Creative Director, threewalls gallery

Threewalls is an artist run gallery and residency space in the West Loop neighborhood of Chicago. It was founded by a group of artists who saw the need for a lasting nonprofit gallery space in Chicago. Shannon is committed to keeping threewalls in close communication with Chicago's creative community and developing it as a healthy, small business. Threewalls also oversees the production and publication of Phonebook, a listing of artist run spaces around North America.

What suggestions do you have for building a sustainable, small organization?
I've noticed there's a lot of resistance to treating artist spaces, resources, or projects like a business. There's an idea that thinking of these projects as a business is capitalist and bad. However, it is possible to scale your growth, create a business plan, look at income and expenses, and create a Board of Directors that is supportive of what you do.

Be clear whether your project is temporary or if you are committed to building an organization long term. Conversely, working three jobs to support your project because you are afraid of thinking of it as a business is not sustainable.

Have patience and don't give up on something you've invested years of your life in building, even if you have not been able to make money at first. It took us five years to be able to hire staff, but we have been in existence for over nine years now. Overall, ensure you are not losing money.

What are some lessons you have learned that you would like to share with others who may be thinking about starting a creative space or community resource?
Know your history and the organizations and ideas that came before you. Every new generation and cycle of people seem to be ignorant of everything that happened before them even though they would be stronger if they learned from those past successes and failures.

Have practical solutions for community needs. Cultivate a community of emotional investors. For example, we offer exhibition opportunities for local artists and invite other local artists to decide who gets shown. When they are involved, people can rally around what you are working on. If you want your business to flourish, make it valuable to as many age groups and types of people as possible.

Build a network of support with people who care about your longevity. It takes a lot of people being involved to make an organization thrive and you have to be open to that involvement for your growth. An organization is not a single person's vision quest.

When you run your own business, you make the roles and culture of your work place. I don't have a boss, I set our workdays, we have a four-day workweek, and we're closed in August. I'm proud of that.

LICENSES, TAXES, PERMITS, ZONING, AND INSURANCE

In addition to incorporating, you may also need a business license to operate. Depending on the type of incorporation you choose you may need to be licensed on the local, state, or federal level in the United States. The Small Business Administration provides links to business licensing agencies in each state and can walk you through what is required.

If you are selling taxable goods, such as crafts or albums, you may also need to apply for a certificate of resale at the state level. This authorizes you to collect and pay sales tax on the items and provide records on all the items you have sold.

Zoning laws are local laws that dictate how certain buildings can be used, whether residential or commercial. If you are running a small mail order zine distribution business out of your living space, zoning may be less of an issue than if you are looking to start a restaurant or open a record store. Before committing to a space for your project find out what laws govern the use of the space.

Insurance protects your event, product or business in case of an accident. It keeps you from being financially liable for damage if an accident is to occur at your space or while someone is using your product. Filmmakers, public performances, and events should all have insurance coverage. If you are renting a space for an event, ask if they extend their insurance coverage to you as part of the package, or if you are required to buy it on your own. There are specific organizations that sell insurance to creative people depending on the industry. When finding an insurance broker you want to be sure they understand what you are doing so that you are charged the correct rate and covered in the event of the unthinkable. There are more insurance resources in the appendix.

PROTECT YOUR RELATIONSHIPS AND CREATIONS: MEMORANDUM OF UNDERSTANDING, CONTRACTS, AND INTELLECTUAL PROPERTY

You've heard the expression "Get it in writing," and whether you have incorporated as a business or are just beginning to collaborate with a partner, a written agreement is essential. An agreement ensures that the terms of your partnership are clear and that you all understand the roles and responsibilities you are taking on.

When working with other people trust and optimism are important, but these should be backed up by a clear contract or memorandum of understanding. An agreement in writing is especially important when you are working with friends. Christen Carter, of Busy Beaver Buttons, advises, "Between friends, trade or give each other discounts on things that you don't do to earn your living, like business advice. Above all, make sure that each of you feel good about the trade and set realistic expectations." Filmmaker William E. Badgley recommends, "When working and negotiating with friends, take care of the business aspects first. Then you know everything you need is in place and you can be social."

If you are working with one person, a group of people, or between organizations once you have decided on the terms of your collaboration, create a "memorandum of understanding," or MOU. An MOU lists the roles and responsibilities of each party involved. Each person signs and dates the completed memo. A MOU may not be legally binding, but it is an important document to have in order to clarify and refer back to in order to understand what everyone is taking on.

Contracts protect relationships and your hard work. An artist once called me in tears because she had co-founded a major literary and arts festival with a friend who had then, after much success, taken complete control and ownership of the project and refused to recognize her co-founder's contributions. They did not have any contracts that identified them as business partners or outlined their responsibilities, which left the artist I spoke with little hope for recourse or recognition for her work, no right to the donations they had raised, and heartbroken about her creative project.

CONTRACT BASICS

A contract keeps the relationship you have forged with a colleague, friend, or collaborator clear and healthy. When you make a contract with a person or organization you are working with, it is an act of respect, empowerment, and courtesy. A good contract clearly spells out each party's obligations and responsibilities. It need not be written in legal language, but must include the following to be considered valid in the United States:

- What the contract is offering

- What each party is expected to do or produce

- The obligation each party has to another

- How payment or exchange will take place

- What will happen if each does not hold up their side of the bargain

For basic contracts, such as between buyers and sellers, or freelancers, you can often find standard language templates online. To enter into a contract both parties must be over 18, be involved out of their own freewill, and be involved in a legal activity. In addition, each party must gain something from the relationship. If one party benefits and the other does not, the exchange is considered a gift.

Empower yourself to understand and be vocal about your needs, whether you are creating a contract or receiving one. Review your contract carefully and make sure you understand each clause. Ask if you do not. If you are entering into a complicated legal agreement, such as a contract with a record company or a film distributor, review your contract with an expert who is knowledgeable in these areas. Any money you pay them for their expertise will save you heartache, pain, and in the long run, money.

PROTECT YOUR INTELLECTUAL PROPERTY

Sharing is an important asset of the do it yourself community. DIY communities are powerful because creative people are generous and are willing to share their ideas and experiences. However, you also want to make sure you protect the unique aspects of your project that you have worked hard to develop. When you make something, whether it's a photograph, piece of music, art, design, or writing, you use a unique combination of your vision, time, expertise, and creativity to realize it.

Your creations are uniquely yours and you deserve to retain the right to say where and how they are used. Musician Greta Gertler, who trained to be a lawyer in her home country of Australia, explains the advantage of understanding intellectual property for creative people, "I've been able to better negotiate deals and find opportunities to sell my work because I understand the value music can have, and how it can be financially rewarding. Many musicians don't want to think about those details, but they need to join organizations that collect performance royalties and understand the contracts they enter into. You are making content and you need to make sure you benefit from what you create."

Guidelines for protecting and respecting intellectual property:

- Ask permission before using someone else's work

- Read and understand the terms of use that web publishing and social media platforms put forth. Many retain rights to images and content you share

- Determine and communicate your terms and conditions for letting others use your creations

- Treat others' property and creation, as you would like them to treat yours. For example, if you want people to purchase your music, buy music from other independent musicians

- Strike a balance between being generous with content and information about your project and undervaluing your work

COPYRIGHT AND TRADEMARK 101

The U.S. Patent Office handles legal property protection in the United States, including Trademarks and Copyright. Trademarks, according the Patent Office, protect words, names, symbols, sounds, or colors that distinguish goods and services. Copyright protects works of authorship, such as writing, music, and works of art. The Library of Congress registers copyrights, which last the life of the author plus 50 years. The U.S. Patent Office offers different options for registering a Trademark or Copyright, including the ability to Copyright materials as a group, which can be a cost effective and efficient option for artists.

An alternative to Copyright is Creative Commons licensing, which allows the creator greater control over how their creation is used, while still maintaining authorship and stipulating specific uses. Creative Commons is a nonprofit that provides license templates and guidelines on how to share and properly make sure you benefit from what you create.

FAIR USE

As a creative person it is important to have a familiarity with Fair Use laws. This is especially important for musicians who use samples in their work, artists working in collage, or filmmakers who want to use clips of other films or music. Fair Use enables creatives to use someone else's intellectual property without attaining permission first. Whether something constitutes "fair use" or not can often be subtle, but in general, copyrighted materials fall under fair use if that use is for teaching, commentary, criticism, reporting, or research.

According to the U.S. Copyright Office there are four tenets of Fair Use:

1. The purpose and character of the use, including whether such use is of commercial nature or is for nonprofit, educational purposes.
2. The nature of the copyrighted work.
3. The amount and substantiality of the portion used in relation to the copyrighted work as a whole.
4. The effect of the use upon the potential market for, or value of, the copyrighted work.

To help negotiate the vague areas of Fair Use check out the book *Reclaiming Fair Use: How to Put the Balance Back in Copyright* put out by the Center for Social Media in 2011.

CONCLUSION: KNOW WHAT YOU NEED TO GROW

Finding the right legal structure for your business, formalizing your relationships with your collaborators, and protecting yourself through purchasing insurance and registering Trademarks or Copyright will create a solid, legal groundwork for your project or business. Personally, it is a challenge to concentrate on these kinds of details, but I know when I have taken care of the business aspects of my creative projects I can move forward with confidence. Work business research and planning into your timeline and set-aside time each week or month to deal with the details.

The business and legal side of your project should be just as beautiful and creative as the artistic side. When you have done this hard work you can have the confidence to know that you are covered should anything go wrong, or, even better, when things go right. Sometimes success, when not planned for, can be the most complicating factor of all."
-William E. Bagley

CHAPTER 4 CHECKLIST

- Acknowledge that when you launch your project you are launching a business

- Choose the legal entity that matches the mission and goals of your business

- Get all agreements in writing

- Understand intellectual property laws and Fair Use to protect yourself and your creation

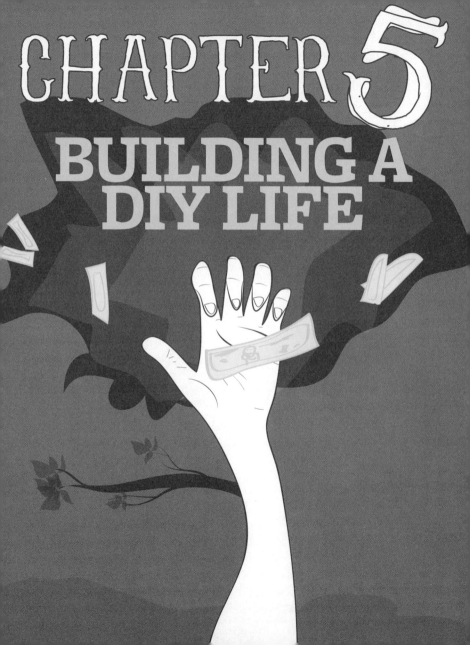

CHAPTER 5

BUILDING A DIY LIFE

EMBARKING on a do it

yourself project is an opportunity to create the life you want to live. Building a DIY life is a process that takes time and conscious effort. You will need to develop healthy work habits, create a lifestyle that nurtures your project, and build collaborations with other do it yourselfers that are productive and inspiring, and participate in a strong, supportive community.

Once you have gotten a handle on the practical and logistical aspects of your project you can figure out how to integrate it into the rest of your life and make your vision a reality. Let's think about managing your work habits, staying motivated through challenging times, strategies for growing your business while staying DIY, and how to productively and creatively work with other people to create a thriving do it yourself community.

NURTURE HEALTHY WORK HABITS

"When you take on a do it yourself project, in that moment, you are deciding your own future," said filmmaker and musician William E. Badgley. If you have read this far you understand that taking your project to the next level requires organization and hard work. Finding a balance between procrastination and pushing yourself to the point of exhaustion as you work on your project requires self-knowledge and striking a careful balance. You'll need to know yourself well to be successful. Take a moment to assess your work habits and skill set. Where might you need to make a change to achieve greater success?

Assess yourself:

- How do you approach a big project? Do you jump in and start working, do you plan, or do you put it off until the last minute?

- How organized are you? Do you have papers everywhere and forget dates or is your mind like a steel trap and your desk as neat as a pin? Do you know how to create organization systems that work for you?

- Are you able to communicate your needs and ask others for help?

- Are you comfortable negotiating? Do you engage in or avoid conversations about responsibility and money?

- How do you respond to feedback? Do you take it personally or look to see how you can improve your project?

Once you understand your strengths and weaknesses, decide what changes you need to make to lay the groundwork for project success. Sometimes that means learning a new skill, changing your schedule, or adjusting your attitude. Amy Cuevas Schroeder, founder of the DIY Business

Association and *Venus Zine*, explained that she had to teach herself to be organized because when she started *Venus Zine* she was known as "Ms. Disorganization."

I used to be unable to say "No" to a new project. When I was in college I took a full course load, worked on the student newspaper, was involved in campus and community organizing, published a zine, worked for an artist, volunteered at a school, and played in a band, as well as worked on the Portland Zine Symposium and taught zine making and book binding workshops in the summers. As a result I was stressed out and busy all the time. I was unable to fully concentrate on my projects or give them my best time and work. I was forced to realize that my commitments were not making me happy and that I had to choose carefully with my time in order to create my best work and get the most out of being involved with the DIY community.

Whether its time management or organization, be clear on the skills you need to improve and be confident that you can change habits to benefit your project.

MAKE YOUR PROJECT A PRIORITY IN YOUR LIFE

Create a lifestyle that supports your project. Develop a space, time, and routine that enables you to be creative. Adjust your schedule to dedicate time to work on your project. While she had a full-time job, in addition to editing her publication *Remedy Quarterly* and blog *The Best Remedy,* Kelley Carambula found she worked best in the morning and focused on her own projects before going to work. "Figure out when you have the most energy and creativity," she advised, "Getting work done on your own projects makes you feel free."

I also work best in the early mornings. To balance my personal writing and projects, a full time job, and freelance work I set up a schedule that includes personal writing in the early morning, work during the day, freelance projects and meetings on weekday evenings. I found I needed the weekends to relax and be social in order to maintain my focus and productivity during the week. After a weekend of seeing my friends and taking care of myself I find I'm excited for Mondays and the time I have made to do the work I love. Knowing my own personal schedule and how much work I am realistically capable of accomplishing also helps me better assess what kind of projects to take on and the timeframe in which I will be able to complete them.

Building a strong foundation for your creative project can be a long process. "Dealing with the administrative aspect of creative projects takes time," says Kelly Carambula, "There are so many details to take care of, but you have to be passionate about them and be prepared to do the dirty work." Musician Greta Gertler agrees and reminds DIY creatives that they need to shift constantly between creation and administration. "Know just because you are stopping the creation aspect for a little while to work on the administrative side of your project doesn't mean your creative work goes away," she said.

"I think of my work promoting my band as a job that I have hired myself to do. Thinking of my musician-self and my promoter-self as different people makes the business side easier." -Alejandra O'Leary

Musician Alejandra O'Leary had to shift her attitude in order to approach the business management aspects of being a do it yourself musician proactively.

To balance his work as a writer and serving as the Executive Director of the Independent Publishing Resource Center, Justin Hocking wrote a personal strategic plan. The IPRC had just been though a strategic planning process that examined the context, goals, needs, and resources available to the organization. Justin went through a similar planning process for his writing career. He found the process useful because, "I learned to delegate, not do everything myself, and find time to be creative and have solo time to work on my writing," he said.

Empowering yourself to embrace the whole responsibility for your project is a unique aspect to the do it yourself community. "A DIY project is a responsibility that you live every day and that is wholly yours," said William E. Badgley. DIY projects can be challenging, but Badgley advises, "Be in love with your project. You will have doubts and rough times, but if you are married to your idea you will not leave it."

KEEP YOUR PROJECT IN PERSPECTIVE

Excitement, enthusiasm, and personal drive to succeed are what nurture successful do it yourself projects. Because your project relies on you to achieve its potential it is imperative to keep yourself healthy. When you keep a positive attitude and close ties with your friends and family, even during intense times, they will help your project grow sustainably.

"You can work around the clock to start a new endeavor," says Greta Gertler, "You need to factor in time apart from your creative passion to relax. This is important for your project to be sustainable. By pursuing your vision you are finding your own path in life, and you want to maintain a sense of well-being."

There may be times when you are not able to step away from your project. It is still possible to keep it in perspective, keep yourself engaged in your project and take care of yourself. Christen Carter passed along advice from her business mentor, "Don't look for balance when growing your business because trying to find balance will stress you out even more. Instead, find things that make you happy and relaxed and will let your brain off the hook."

Do it yourself does not have to mean "do it alone." Your project can be an opportunity to nurture relationships with friends and family. Talk with them about your project, what it makes you think about, and how it makes you feel. You want the people you are close to in your life to be there to understand, cheer you on, and celebrate your success with you.

To keep your project in perspective, revisit your goals, vision, and mission. Assess:

- Are your goals and timeline realistic based on what else is going on in your life?

- Are you making enough time for your project and for your friends, family, and yourself? Why or why not?

- What about your project do you love? Why do you love that part of it?

- What about your project do you want to change?

- Is your project going according to plan? If not, how do you need to re-do your timeline or re-think your goals?

- What are the good things that your project brings to your life?

When times are difficult, being able to consistently see the forest through the trees is essential. Maintaining a bigger perspective will power you through tasks that you find less rewarding. Shannon Stratton, of threewalls, reminds artists, organizers, and creatives, "Lose that flashpoint mentality and stick to the thing you believe in. Hone it, polish it, work at it and believe someone will notice eventually, but not immediately. Fame is not instant. It is your persistence that will bring you and your project to a tipping point."

BUILD HEALTHY COLLABORATIONS

The success of your project ultimately depends how well you work with others. I have a lot of ideas for projects I want to accomplish, but have found that my initial ideas are made better by sharing them and shaping them with other creative people. Working on collaborative projects has enabled me to realize ideas that are much larger than what

I could accomplish alone, such as a weekend long zine symposium or publishing two issues of a queer, feminist art journal and hosting a series of events around its release. Some projects are more collaborative in nature than others. For example, in my band we all work together to write songs, whereas my zines tend to be only about me and my personal, creative vision. However, no mater how solitary your project, at some point you will need to work with others to achieve your goals.

Collaboration is important because it enables you to delegate, share, and balance the tasks that you need to complete to accomplish your project. The first two years of the Portland Zine Symposium I took on a major coordinating role that involved overseeing everything from printing programs to making food for participants to coordinating and leading workshops. At first I resisted delegating the responsibilities I had taken on to other symposium planning committee members and volunteers because I feared that the necessary work would not get done. I have found this is a common mistake among creative people who fear letting go of any responsibility will hurt their project. However, when I finally let go of some control and let others take a leadership role on specific tasks I found that those tasks got done more effectively. By collaborating with others I was able to focus on the aspects of the symposium that I was really good at and interested in, such as planning and coordinating workshops, and gave others the chance to contribute their skills and enthusiasm to the event.

Before initiating a collaboration, assess your strengths and weaknesses to identify what aspects of your project will benefit by working with someone whose talents complement yours. I always find that when I work with inspiring people I have a greater amount motivation and energy to realize my project.

Before you enter into a collaboration, Christen Carter, Founder of Busy Beaver Buttons, advises, "Understand your core competencies. What you are really good at? If you need to hire people, find people who are complementary to you so that you get all that you need and create a win-win situation for everyone involved." Antonio Ramos of Brooklyn Soda Works concurs, "It is important to hire and work with a range of people who bring different skill sets and different ideas."

Justin Hocking, Executive Director of the Independent Publishing Resource Center, weighs in on the importance of collaboration for do it yourself projects and organizations. "The idea of 'do everything your self' can be misleading. DIY is great when you are starting out and need creative alone time, but you need help when you run a business. Too many businesses fail because people don't bring in other people to help them do the things that make it possible for them to create. If you are a leader of an organization you need to do high level strategizing. If you are bogged down in every tiny detail of running the business, it will exhaust you."

It takes time, planning, and effort to build successful collaborations and rewarding partnerships that help your business run effectively. Collaborations must be carefully cultivated and nurtured to be sustainable.

Guidelines for healthy collaboration:

- Work with people whose talents and skills complement yours

- Be honest about your strengths and weaknesses

- Communicate your needs, expectations, hopes, and fears

- Be clear about what you want out of the collaboration

- Define each partners' roles in writing

- Give back as much as you are getting out of the collaboration

- Check in with your partners and reassess the collaboration regularly

When you work with other people you will be able to grow your project into a sustainable business. Justin Hocking reminds creatives that, "When you work with someone it's like a marriage and marriages are not easy." While it takes effort to collaborate, every interaction can open a new door for you, so treat the relationships you forge with others with respect and seriousness.

NURTURE DIY COMMUNITY

Community and relationships are some of the most important resources that do it yourself, creative people have to offer one another. Being an active participant in your community will build goodwill and support for your project. Goodwill is the strongest currency that you have to offer.

I feel that my life has been a testament to the power of do it yourself community. The success I've been able to achieve with my projects has been thanks to the communities that surround me. When I lived in Portland, Maine in the late-1990s there were very few venues or bookers for independent and punk bands. Because I played in bands and booked our shows I made a conscious effort to help out bands from out of town who wanted to play in Maine. As a result, when my band went on a tour of the East Coast there were many bands that offered us a show in their town or connected us with other friends in return and the work of booking a tour became a reason to be in touch with friends instead of a stressful chore. Several years later, when I needed help to produce 300 copies of a zine that had a complicated hand binding I asked others in the zine community to help me and offered them a bookbinding lesson and homemade snacks in return. I turned a project that would have taken me many solitary days alone at my desk to complete into a community-oriented skill-share.

Community is the element that sets DIY businesses and projects apart from other types of creative business. Justin Hocking, says, "Do it yourself is the impetus for starting things. Community is what sustains them." If you position yourself as a responsible community member who cares about others you will never have to look far for help or support as your project grows.

Build connections to other DIY businesses or creative people so they can serve as sources of advice, support, and inspiration as your project develops. They understand what you are going through because they have had similar experiences. This support is crucial if you plan to make your project into a full-time job. Antonio Ramos of Brooklyn Soda Works explained that when they were developing their soda making process they relied on the advice and experience of the home brewing community. He reminds those with DIY business ambitions, "You are not the first person to do this. Seek out advice from those who have gone before you. Take an idea or technique someone else uses and adapt it to your needs."

When you are in touch with your community you will be able to fully recognize and celebrate your successes and find new approaches when the going gets tough. I try to build community through simple acts like going to events other like-minded creative people organize, donating to crowd funding campaigns (even if just a little bit to show I care), helping to spread the word about projects that interest me, and keeping in touch and following through with people that I meet. To further deepen DIY community, Christen Carter recommends forming roundtables, support sessions, and regular meet ups with other DIY business owners and project creators to share advice, help each other set goals and reflect on your progress and process. When you get together with like-minded community members you can create resources that each other can use, such as skill-sharing or bartering sessions.

Community building events can be fun and productive. For example, my friend Laura Leebove, editor of the food and music blog *Eating the Beats*, and I started a "creative lady" potluck dinner where we invited creative women we knew who did not yet know each other. We instructed each person to bring a similarly creative friend and over dinner we each shared what we were working on and our goals for taking the next step with our projects. We gathered every four months and our dinners were an opportunity to check in with each other and hold each other accountable to our goals in a relaxed, social setting.

Position yourself as a participant in the DIY community. When you engage your passion to grow a project you will develop strong feelings and opinions. As you find ways to express your ideas through your project and passion, always remember the golden rule: treat people as you would expect to be treated.

"Practice what you know, be who you are and don't alienate people who can help you. Understand when to compromise and watch out for those impulses that would cause you to burn bridges," advised Tim Haft of Punk Rope. When you participate in the DIY community you have an opportunity to cultivate your capacity for compassion, respect, and patience. Give feedback and don't shy away from constructive criticism of others work if they ask you, but work to frame your feedback as being squarely about someone's project or business, not as a critique of them personally. I have grown immensely from feedback I've received from writers and editors I have worked with and participants at events I organized. However, I've also witnessed the breakdown of community when feedback about a project such as a zine, band, or event has devolved into judgments about someone's character, identity, or history. Personally, when I was younger, I made the mistake of saying less than complimentary things about another zine maker's writing and personality and had to apologize profusely and take time to rebuild our relationship before they would trust me again. From that experience I learned that before you make a judgment, take your time to get to know your peers and understand their perspective. Remember, no one is perfect and everyone grows and changes with their project.

The network you develop in the DIY community is crucial for the life of your project. As you grow your project you will find more opportunities to call on those in your network for their expertise and support. Keep those relationships as healthy as possible.

Your sense of self-awareness is an asset to the DIY community. When you understand your background and the perspective that you come from you will be able to connect with people who have had different experiences from your own. Take time and effort to understand the background and cultural context that others come from. Be humble, honest, and willing to discuss the privileges you have grown up with, the opportunities you have been given and created for yourself, and the challenges you have faced. It is not always comfortable or easy to have these conversations, but when you do so people will appreciate and respect you more for it.

Take care of yourself mentally and physically so that you can take care of your project and the community that nurtures it. Filmmaker William E. Badgley shared a basic rule for being a responsible community member. "Keep yourself healthy. If you are healthy you will inspire health in others."

FOUR ELEMENTS OF A SUCCESSFUL, DIY COMMUNITY PROJECT

Sarah Evans, co-founder of the Roberts Street Social Centre, Halifax NS

When starting a project with a group of people, these are some guidelines to keep it focused, useful, and interesting for all involved.

1. Start small and simple. Have a kernel of a great idea or identify a need to fill. Stay focused. A simple project will get you started. The rest will come in ways you can't predict.
2. Collaborate with people who have different sets of skills. It's awesome to bring together people with diverse interests.
3. Plan your project out, but don't plan too much. If planning does not feel useful then focus on implementing your ideas and making them happen.
4. Remember what you have done and learn from it: "I can do anything if I was able to accomplish that" is a great feeling to have. When you start a project you gain confidence and determination and you can use those feelings to launch other, larger projects, or grow your current project.

ORGANIZING AND RUNNING A COLLECTIVE: SARAH EVANS AND THE ROBERTS STREET SOCIAL CENTRE

Collectives are created from collaboration on a deep, sustained level. The collective is a model for running a project or organization that divides responsibility and ownership between members. Collectives' strength comes from the fact that they bring together people with different skills, expertise, and ideas to create an entity that has a larger impact than what those individuals could achieve on their own. Collectives often have a mission and a shared set of values that govern their activities and decision-making. They have regular meetings where decisions that are important to the project are made as a group and tasks are delegated to different members.

Sarah Evans is an artist and activist from Canada. From 2005 to 2011 she helped found and run the Roberts Street Social Centre, an artist residency, workshop space, and printing studio in Halifax, Nova Scotia. The center served local students and community groups, as well as independent publishers, activists, and artists from Halifax and beyond. The Centre started because the founders, "Were really into the possibilities and relationships that a space could foster. We wanted to create a project based around art and activism without becoming an entity that was easily defined. We wanted to bring people together in the city and act as a resource for folks visiting."

Sarah and her co-founder Sonia formed a collective to make decisions about how the center was run. They created a process for consensus decision-making and held monthly collective meetings where all were invited to participate. Sarah explained that they continued to adjust the policies as more people got involved and the center grew.

Working successfully with a collective
Sarah Evans

- Ensure you share a common goal and vision

- Keep it friendly. Have opportunities for folks to get to know each other outside of meetings

- Build a dedicated membership so that you can accomplish the tasks you need

- Foster autonomy for members so they can exercise their judgment and do what they think is best for the project

- Use collective decision making to steer the bigger picture and make significant decisions

- Create policies to work through divisive issues before they arise

Sarah Evans reminds those starting collectives that the process is both extremely rewarding and very difficult. Before embarking on a collective project check in with those involved about your goals and timeline: Do you plan to create a long term, sustainable community resource or are you coming together for a specific, short term purpose? Your mission, policies, structure, and the roles each member takes on will vary depending on your reason for coming together. For example, when I worked on the Portland Zine Symposium a new planning committee formed each year and worked together to realize that year's event, whereas the Radical Art Girls was an ongoing group that came together around a shared set of values and worked on different projects driven by those values. A successful collective realizes a group vision without compromising the unique skill-sets, voice, and perspective of each member.

THE BUSINESS OF DIY:ARE YOU READY TO DO IT YOURSELF FULL-TIME?

Whether you are working on your project collectively, in a partnership, or on your own, your dreams will start to become reality. The beauty of do it yourself projects is that you can choose the level of engagement that you want to have with them. How big your project becomes depends on your goals. As you accomplish the initial goals you set for your project you may find that it is becoming bigger, and more successful than you first imagined and demanding more of your time.

You may have launched your project because you wanted a way to hone an interest outside of your professional life, to bring more creativity into your work, or create a sustainable business that supports your lifestyle. Whatever your reasons, if your project grows to demand a full-time commitment, there are important personal and financial aspects to consider before you take the leap to make your project your full time job.

It is exciting, scary, and exhilarating to venture out on your own. You will need an emotional and financial basis of support for your transition into professional do it yourselfer. It is a shift in your lifestyle that you want to be prepared for because it will change your life in ways that you don't yet expect.

In *Rookie* magazine Jessica Hopper asks those interested in starting their own business, "What is your contingency plan [if your business doesn't work out]? Scale back? Ask for help? Lots of time, people want to jump into their business full time, right away. Working up to that conservatively and organically is a much safer bet; there is nothing wrong with starting (very) small."

Before taking the plunge, ease into working for yourself if you have never done so before. Before leaving her full-time job as a graphic designer to concentrate on her magazine *Remedy Quarterly*, her blog, and other projects, Kelly Carambula cut her hours at her day job to build up her projects and took on freelance clients outside of work. When she was ready to make the transition she already had freelance clients lined up and a magazine and blog with a developed audience.

Prepare for full-time DIY

FROM A PERSONAL PERSPECTIVE:

- Ensure you have the self-discipline necessary to impose and meet timelines and deadlines.

- Do you need a community around you when you work? If so, where will you find this?

- Tell your friends and family about your decision and build a support network for your work/life transition. Identify the people who will listen to you and support you when the going gets tough.

- Identify and reach out to a mentor. Find someone who has done something similar before and is enthusiastic about sharing their knowledge with you.

- If you have a job, you may want to talk about your decision with your employer and ensure that you leave your job as professionally, politely, and with as much goodwill as possible. You never know when you will work together again and in what capacity.

- Make a plan to balance your new, self-directed employment with your personal life.

- Contact your network of friends, family, supporters, and fans and let them know you are making the transition to full-time DIY so they can hire you and help spread the word about your project.

FROM A FINANCIAL AND LOGISTICAL PERSPECTIVE:

- Know your monthly business and personal expenses. If you work for yourself your project(s) will need to cover both.

- Ensure your project is making enough money to cover the costs it incurs.

- Build up your savings in advance to cover living expenses while you transition to working on your project full-time.

- Assess your lifestyle: Are your spending priorities in line with growing your project or starting a business?

- Prepare to cover the additional expenses of working for yourself. You will be responsible for your health insurance, taxes, and overhead expenses like office rent and supplies.

- Identify your ideal work style and environment. Find workspaces that fit your needs.

In the resources section of this book there are places where you can find low-cost co-working spaces and other options for taking care of the logistical and practical needs of your new business or growing project.

If you are ready to take the plunge, congratulations! Going out on your own is a risk and the ability and desire to do so is different for everyone. Kelly Carambula suggests you let yourself be inspired by the risk takers around you until you are ready to take that risk yourself. Greta Gertler counsels, "Allow yourself a few months of not earning very much money. If you can get by and devote a block of time to your project it will open up a whole new life that's really rewarding."

When Brooklyn Soda Works became his full-time job, Antonio Ramos noticed a shift in his approach to the business. "When you are full time there are more demands. You need to be stricter and implement austerity measures. You need to work harder to have a self-sustaining business."

As you push yourself into new personal, creative, and professional territory acknowledge and celebrate your accomplishments. When you recognize how your project has developed you will gain perspective and confidence. The reward for hard work, creative thinking, and careful decision-making is a future of your own making, custom built for and by yourself.

LETTING YOUR BUSINESS GROW

Like collaboration, growing your do it yourself project into a business takes time and careful planning. Think carefully as you scale up your business, whether that means finding new customers or more places to sell your work, increasing the capacity of your business, or making new products. Assess what additional resources you require and how growing will enhance your vision for your DIY business. Find help if you need it, whether that means working with volunteers or interns from local universities for class credit; working with a lawyer, accountant, or other professionals to handle tasks you cannot do yourself; or hiring employees to work with you. Working with other people to grow your business will bring a new dynamic to the work you do. Jessica Hopper instructs those starting and growing their own business, "Don't expect people to work more hours than you pay them for. Don't expect people to pledge their souls (and/or free time) to your endeavors. Don't expect them to care as much as you do about whether the business survives."

GUIDELINES FOR SUSTAINABLE DIY BUSINESS GROWTH

From Christen Carter, Founder and CEO, Busy Beaver Buttons

Busy Beaver Buttons began over 15 years ago in Christen Carter's college dorm room and is responsible for re-popularizing the one-inch button. Thanks to Christen's dedication, vision, and commitment to customer service, they have built a stable business with multiple employees. Plus, she gets to do what she loves, connect ideas and people by making items that help share these ideas through wearable graphics. Christen shared her experiences with growing sustainably and working with others successfully:

- Make your customers happy, give them what they need, and let them know you are on their side.

- Approach growing your business as an artistic process: What materials do you need and how and who do you need to grow to support this process?

- Protect yourself and your time: Require customers to pre-pay as much as you can.

- Beware of extremes in pricing: Do not offer so many discounts you can't stay in business, while still being fair.

- Recognize when you can't do it all yourself and acknowledge that you are part of a larger community.

- Work with mentors that will keep you on track, light a fire under you, and share their wisdom and experiences.

- Bring in experts for specific business needs, such as human resources, accounting, or law.

- If you have employees, work collaboratively to set goals and set up a human resource infrastructure so everyone feels supported.

- Do your own emotional work to understand what you are doing and why.

REFLECT, REASSESS, AND STAY MOTIVATED

When you build a creative, do it yourself life, project, or business you are sending a message that you believe in yourself and your creative vision. You are going against the grain of what is expected of your work, life, and career. Not everyone will share that vision and you will encounter resistance at times. In order to stay motivated about your project, take time to reassess it honestly and define what it brings to your life.

Take time to acknowledge your creativity and your own needs. Justin Hocking warns, "There can be a martyr syndrome in the DIY community and people can fall into the trap of, 'I am doing it for the good of the community,' but you should think about how you design your job and your life around your own creative work."

Commit to your project, your vision, and yourself. Remember the bigger picture when challenges arise. Musician Alejandra O'Leary suggests, "As a DIY artist, learn to think of yourself as a long term investment and keep short term successes and failures in perspective. Prepare to do things for the long haul."

I've worked to slowly build my freelance writing portfolio since I graduated from college. While sometimes I feel like I just have random clips here or there, when I step back I can see how my writing developed over time, that I began to write more consistently for larger venues, and that I have developed a diverse portfolio. By taking a longer focus I can see and feel a sense of progress.

If you are getting bored with your project find ways to change it up and make routine tasks more interesting. Work in a different space, make a regular work date with a friend, or get a group together for a work party on a particular repetitive task. Set goals for completing small tasks and reward yourself for meeting these goals.

If you find yourself hitting a wall and losing inspiration and motivation, step away from your project for a while. You are your own worst critic and harshest deadline keeper. Be generous to yourself and take a break so that you can come back to your project with a fresh perspective. Stepping away can strengthen your project. Kelly Carambula noted, "When you have experiences outside of your project they enable you to be open to new ideas and inspiration."

THE LIFE CYCLE OF A PROJECT

Do it yourself projects can come to an end but still be considered a success. The creative process of launching a project and building a business is not straightforward. Along the way you will encounter opportunities, challenges, and new ideas that will change your course and alter your carefully laid plans.

Part of building a successful, creative project is to know when it has run its course. If your project is an event, exhibition, or object like a film or book, it may have a natural end point. If you are running a collective, building a movement, or starting a business, the end may be less obvious. Tim Haft, of Punk Rope, advised, "If you've been doing what you're doing and it has hit a plateau or declined, accept that its not going any further or make a change. Instead of looking at it as failure, find a way to pivot gracefully."

In order to grow, there came a time when I had to step away from the Portland Zine Symposium. My life had become more oriented towards New York City and less towards Portland, Oregon. I was concentrating more on teaching and community organizing and less on making zines and participating in the zine community. The Symposium felt more like an obligation than a pleasure. I knew that a solid enough basis of support for the event had been established that I could decrease my involvement and the event would continue to grow and develop.

After spending almost four years working on *riffRAG*, a queer feminist art magazine, the three other editors and I decided to end the project and move on. We enjoyed working together, but became more focused on our individual, creative pursuits that included filmmaking, art making, and playing music. In addition, I realized that while I had began the project because I did not regularly engage with feminist art as much as I wanted to, by the time the project ended I was teaching about and putting together public programming focused on feminist art and artists at a New York City art museum as my full time job. I realized that in my free time I needed to focus my creativity on a different set of ideas and issues.

Sometimes a project is a great idea, but once you start to implement it you may find that you do not have the resources or time to realize it fully. My friend Tracy Candido and I worked to start a supper club called "Eat Art" that combined our love of facilitating conversations about contemporary art and cooking original, seasonally inspired recipes. Tracy had a strong history of similar projects that had gotten a lot of attention from local media. We thought that launching a project centered around artisanal food in Brooklyn would hit the right audience, because the borough has a robust community that is interested in local food events. However, we found that the members of the media found the art and food message difficult to promote, that the logistics of finding a space and kitchen to create and serve the meal were daunting, and that the price to purchase food and secure space was higher than we had initially calculated. As a result, we decided to cancel our initial dinner and rethink the series of events we had planned. After much reflection and assessment Tracy and I ultimately decided we did not have the resources we needed to continue the project, especially given our other commitments. It was a difficult decision because we both felt very passionate about the project. However, we did learn that we worked very well together and have collaborated on a number of smaller projects and events since then.

Just like people and communities, a creative project needs to change, grow, and evolve. When to wrap up, pass on, or pivot a project is wholly up to you and how you feel about it. What is necessary and appropriate are often feelings from the gut that you will know innately as an extension of your vision. But accepting that it is time to throw in the towel is not always easy.

CONSIDERATIONS FOR ENDING OR SHIFTING A PROJECT:

- Is your project a source of joy and motivation? Why or why not?

- Does the project feel overly burdensome on your time?

- Is the project still relevant to the community or culture that it serves?

- Has the reason you started the project changed?

- Have the needs and interests of project partners or collaborators shifted?

- Is the project losing money or are you going into debt?

If it is time to end or fundamentally change your project, think carefully. You have invested a lot of time, energy, and thought. Ensure that your reputation, the identity that you have built, and the network you have cultivated stays intact after you make that transition. If you feel your project can and should continue without you, make a plan to pass it on to someone else. Be prepared to let your responsibility go and trust the person who is taking it on. If you decide to pivot your project to follow a new direction, rewrite your mission, vision, and goals, rethink your identity to reflect that new approach. If the problems with the project are purely financial, identify the expenses you need to cut and make a plan to find more support to make the project happen. This can be surprisingly hard emotionally, especially after many years, because DIY projects are very much about yourself as well as the project. Take the time to identify, share, and process your feelings.

When you shift a project you ensure that you continue to build on your past success and open the door to future opportunities. Take time to reflect on what you have accomplished, document what you have learned, and understand how the project and you have changed. No matter where you end up, the time, energy, and expertise you put into and gain from your do it yourself endeavor will always lay the ground work for what's next and help you grow.

TIPS FOR BUILDING YOUR DIY PROJECT, BUSINESS, AND LIFE:

- Assess your skills and be honest about your strengths and weaknesses

- Cultivate a space, time and routine that maximizes your creativity

- Think of yourself, and your project, as a long term investment

- Value the DIY community

- Clearly define your goals and expectations when working with other people

- Communication creates healthy collaboration

- Goodwill is your most valuable asset

- Regularly assess your project and your feelings about it to decide when its time to grow, pivot, or move on

- Be persistent and build the life that you dream of

IN CONCLUSION:
EMBRACE YOUR DIY PRESENT AND FUTURE. DARE TO GROW

When you decide to do it yourself you take a risk to be creative, empowered, and fulfilled. Your project may last one year, ten years, or a lifetime, but no matter what the timeframe, your accomplishments and the community you build will impact your life in surprising ways. When you start a DIY project you create an opportunity to shape your life how you want it and participate in the wider culture and economy on your own terms. When you embrace DIY you open yourself to a broader network and community. When you choose to go DIY you challenge your assumptions and expectations in order to discover the many possibilities available to you to help support your project.

My engagement with the do it yourself community began with making zines and playing in a band. As I've grown my career around supporting creative people and organized larger community events I chose to keep a do it yourself approach to my life, which has opened me to a wider understanding of what DIY is and can be. On a daily basis I talk to musicians, techies, filmmakers, community organizers, artists, foodies, crafters, and writers, among others, who are all working to make a sustainable life that supports their creativity, helps others and adds value to the world. I have found that once they take a risk to connect to a larger community their projects are able to achieve greater success.

By staying involved in DIY I have discovered a lot about myself. I found that I value independence and my own economic self-determination, as well as working for larger organizations that serve a wide community and are able to have a larger impact than what I could achieve on my own. Collaboration and being open to feedback, new ideas, and broader perspectives has strengthened my work. Being involved in the DIY community has shown me, in a very practical way, that I can construct my life how I chose. I know that if I identify a creative goal the responsibility rests squarely on me, and the network of support I build, to accomplish it.

For several years after I finished college I spent my time wishing I were a writer, instead of writing. I felt there were others in my community who had achieved the success that I felt should be possible for me. At first I felt jealous. Then I remembered why I started making zines in the first place: I wanted to be a writer. No one gives permission or validation to build a career as a writer or to take on any creative endeavor; I simply had to start. I broke down the steps I needed to take, brainstormed subjects in which I was interested and had expertise, and identified publications to pitch stories to. I've worked slowly and steadily to develop my technique, build my portfolio, and strengthen my confidence in my writing. I've built a community of zinesters's who became writers, editors, and publishers, and networked with creative people that I would like to write about. I have a long way to go, but I can trace my confidence in my personal creative practice directly to my involvement with the DIY community.

We are living in an exciting time for DIY because, thanks to technology, new free and cost-efficient tools and sharing mechanisms that help independent, creative people do their jobs are made available every day. Challenge and empower yourself to find the answers to your questions and the support that you need.

Creative projects that address community needs, express creative ideas, and present imaginative solutions to common problems enrich our culture and economy. When you take the leap to launch a DIY project or business you choose to add value to your life and the lives of your friends, family, and community. You demonstrate that our culture is diverse, interesting, and surprising and show there are alternatives to a mainstream culture of work and consumption that values profit over people and following the rules over innovation.

You have the tools and the creative capacity to realize your dream project. Reach out, build community, make a plan, take a deep breath, and get started. It's up to you to create the life and success that you dream of.

RESOURCES

Find the resources you need to be successful and sustainable. *Grow* is a gateway for you to access the world of resources that are available for your specific project. These are some favorite resources that the interviewees in this book and I have found helpful and inspiring.

Career And Business Planning

the $100 startup: reinvent they way you make a living, do what you love, and create a new future chris guillebeau
a fun, innovative guide to launching and growing a business on your terms

the artists guide: making a living doing what you love jackie battenfield
excellent career planning guide for all types of creative people

art/work: everything you need to know (and do) as you pursue your art career heather darcy bhandari and jonathan melber
practical considerations for launching your career as an artist

come hell or high-water richard singer
how to create and work in a collective environment

craft, inc. meg mateo ilasco
turning your creative hobby into a business

creative, inc. joy deangdeelert cho and meg mateo ilasco
planning and organizing your freelance career

getting your sh*t together (gyst)
www.gyst-ink.com
artist-run company that offers free and paid resources for creative people to manage the business aspects including sales, proposals, inventory, and mailing lists that offers software, services, and workshops

the handmade marketplace kari chapin
how to launch a craft business

music success in nine weeks ariel hyatt
guide to setting goals and achieving them for bands and musicians

Money, Finance, And Fundraising
the creative professional's guide to money ilise benun
accessible advice for managing your money

the crafter's guide to pricing your work dan ramsey

the foundation center
www.foundationcenter.org and grantspace.org
extensive database for researching grants from public and private institutions. offers classes, workshops, and resources for learning about fundraising, including sample proposals

the graphic artists guild handbook: pricing & ethical guidelines
invaluable information about contracts, pricing, and legal rights for graphic artists

indiegogo
www.indiegogo.com
international crowd funding platform to raise money for creative, community, and activist projects

kicksarter
www.kickstarter.com
crowd funding platform for creative projects

mint.com
www.mint.com
free online personal finance, budget planning, and money management program

rockethub
www.rockethub.com
creative, community-oriented crowd funding platform that provides extensive information on how to set up a crowd funding campaign and connects creatives to greater opportunities

wave accounting
www.waveaccounting.com
free online accounting software for small businesses

Community Building, Networking, Marketing, Online Presence, and Social Media

cd baby
www.cdbaby.com
an artist run site that is the world's largest online distributor of independent music in all genres

etsy
www.etsy.com
online marketplace for handmade items that offers extensive education and networking resources for its sellers

indie on the move
www.indieonthemove.com
venue listing for touring bands that includes genre, reviews, venue capacity, and booking information

the independent publishing resource center
www.iprc.org
workspace, classes, and community for all types of self-publishers in portland, oregon

media bistro
www.mediabistro.com
membership-based organization offering jobs, community building, courses, and connections for those in creative and content-based fields

phonebook 2011/2012: *a directory of independent art spaces, programming and projects across the united states threewalls*, edited by abigail satinsky

other peoples pixels
www.otherpeoplespixels.com
artist run company that offers template websites for fine artists that includes options for selling your work

wix lounge
www.wixlounge.com and www.wixloungesf.com
wix lounges offer free co-working space, events, and professional development workshops for creatives in new york and san francisco as well as free, template websites for artists

wordpress.com and wordpress.org
resources for building your own website, whether free or paid, with open source software

Legal and Business Support

american society of composers, authors, and publishers (ascap)
www.ascap.com
u.s.-based performance rights organization for musicians and composers

b lab
bcorporation.net
information about forming a social benefit corporation or "b corp"

bmi
www.bmi.com
business that collects licensing fees and distributes royalties for musicians

creative commons
creativecommons.org
nonprofit organization that enables the sharing and use of creativity and knowledge through free legal tools

fractured atlas
www.fracturedatlas.org
professional development, insurance, fiscal sponsorship, and resources for artists in all disciplines

the graphic artists guild
www.graphicartistsguild.org
national networking, advocacy, and professional development organization for graphic artists including designers, illustrators, cartoonists, and digital artists

the legal guide for the visual artist tad crawford
a reference book covering basic legal issues for anyone working in the visual arts

national cooperative business association
www.ncba.coop
information and resources about finding, starting and, working at a cooperative

the new york foundation for the arts
www.nyfa.org and www.artspire.org
resources, professional development, fiscal sponsorship, and information for artists in all disciplines, no matter where they live. for researching grants, services, and opportunities check out nfya source at www.nyfa.org/source

score
www.score.org
nonprofit offering small business counseling and mentoring
small business association
www.sba.gov
support, resources, mentoring, and links to government forms and agencies for those launching or running a small business

u.s. copyright office
www.copyright.gov
register a copyright and find more information about protecting your intellectual property

volunteer lawyers for the arts
www.vlany.org
based in nyc vla offers legal classes, workshops, and advocacy for artists and arts nonprofits

Inspiration, Motivation and Support for Building a DIY Life

brainpickings
www.brainpickings.org
a multidisciplinary site full of inspirational ideas, tools, and techniques for creative people

collabfinder
collabfinder.com
site to help creators and geeks, such as writers, designers, and programmers, connect to collaborate on new projects

the diy business association
diybusinessassociation.com/
content that empowers and connects creative entrepreneurs—because it takes a community to do it yourself.

fast company
www.fastcompany.com
entrepreneurial ideas and inspiration

freelancers union
www.freelancersunion.org/
insurance, advocacy, resources, and support for independent workers

ourgoods
www.ourgoods.org
a barter network for the creative community that helps you barter skills, spaces, and objects

skillshare
www.skillshare.com
a global marketplace for classes

ted
www.ted.com
"ideas worth spreading," talks on a huge variety of subjects for edification and inspiration

ACKNOWLEDGEMENTS

The wise words, "It takes a community to do it yourself," from Amy Cuevas Schroeder have guided me throughout the writing of this book. *Grow* has been an effort truly supported by members of the many different, overlapping creative communities that I have had the privilege to be a part of. When I started making zines and recording my own music as a teenager I never imagined that DIY would become so central to my life. I am thankful to all those whose lives have intersected with mine since that time and all of the lessons you have taught me along the way. It is thanks to the DIY community that this book exists.

I would especially like to extend my gratitude to: Joe Biel and Cantankerous Titles for believing in this idea and nurturing it from the get go. I could not have asked for a better introduction to the world of publishing; Draft readers Tracy Candido, Marisha Chinsky, and Charles Buell for their insight, revisions, and thorough feedback that helped shape this into a real book; Stephanie Rousseau for her beautiful design ideas; John and Sue Clippinger for offering me space for a DIY writer's retreat; Ariel Hyatt, Matt Madden, Cathy Erway, Joshua Ploeg, Heather Darcy Bhandari, Karina Mangu Ward and Laura Leebove for their early support; Amy Cuevas Schroeder for being a tireless advocate, connector, and inspiration; My band mates Marisha Chinsky, Aileen Brophy, and Nick Cearelock for being partners in DIY creativity; Sharif Hassan for his constant support and advice; Lauren Jade Martin for demonstrating how to live an adult DIY life; My parents Mike and Rosemary Whitney who taught me the values of self-reliance, thrift, creativity, and have been tireless supporters of my DIY adventures since the beginning. Special love to my tireless assistant and head of home office motivation, Crackers the cat.

I am especially appreciative to all of the interviewees for giving freely of their time, advice, and expertise. This book would not be the resource it is without them: William E. Badgley, Shana Brady, Christen Carter, Kelly Carambula, Sarah Evans, Temim Fruchter, Greta Gertler, Charlie Grosso, Tim Haft, Justin Hocking, Caroline Mak, Danielle Maveal, Brian Meece, Alejandra O'Leary, Stephanie Rousseau, Amy Cuevas Schroeder, Shannon Stratton, and Antonio Ramos. Thank you to Jessica Hopper for her permission to quote her article "Be Your Own Boss," originally published in *Rookie* Magazine.